# CYCLE SPACE

## Architecture & Urban Design in the Age of the Bicycle

### Steven Fleming

nai010 publishers

Bicycle parked in front of the Cooper Union building, New York, NY
Photo: Steven Fleming

# CYCLE SPACE

Ray and Maria Stata Center, Frank Gehry, 2004, Massachusetts Institute of Technology, Boston
Photo: Steven Fleming

## Navigating
## the City

Just like the post-industrial city, the sky was once something people could only gaze up at, in awe and bewilderment. Once aeroplanes were invented, we didn't have to call it sky anymore. We called it airspace and used it for travel.

Cities can be bewildering too. As drivers, we're relegated to the vortex of the cross-city tunnel, the colour-coded car parking garage and the everywhere bottleneck. As metro users we are but humanity extruded through tubes in the ground. The bus is a rocking asylum. Pedestrians have had no city built for their edification since feudal times. However you move through them, cities assail you. Unless you cycle.

Looking at cities through the idea of 'cycle space' is like applying the term airspace to our skies. It is the first step in the city's demystification. Step two is to simply start cycling, everywhere, day or night, on wet or dry days, to see for yourself the truth of this claim: cycling shrinks cities to roughly the size of big buildings, both in size and complexity. Step three, if you have any say in the way cities are built, planned or governed, is to exercise that volition to reveal the potential of cities for cycling, by making them not only safer, but also more fun in a world where:

- some cyclists want to look all retro on their French porteurs; - others want to look eco and do-it-yourself;
- still others like they just stepped out of the Bauhaus and are too-cool-for-you;
- another lot as though they are leading le Tour;
- some as though they're about to ride off a cliff in their beetle suits;
- and the rest like they don't care at all, dressed in their day-glow – or whatever nerds wear on their bikes.

You know, I can take my coffee at Chelsea Market, post a letter and use a loo at Columbus Circle, drop back by the West Village to pick up my jumper because clouds have come over, be taking calls on my phone and still meet my friend for a late breakfast near Bryant Park, all because I like cycling. Rem Koolhaas's book *Delirious New York* begins as some kind of ode to congestion. But New York isn't congested, as far as I can tell on the folding bike I take there. I get the sense Koolhaas wastes too much of his time when he goes to New York trapped in the back seat of taxis, forgetting this is New Amsterdam after all. I just want to say this, Mr Koolhaas: love your work, but seeing New York with delirium is purely a matter of choice.

New York is just another patch of earth like the rest, where if you lean left you will turn left, and if you lean right you will turn right. Circular motions made with your legs seem to reel Broadway towards you, then beneath you, then out behind you, as you cross from SoHo to the East Village. It's as simple as that. Bikes give you this sense of control and reorientation.

## Cities Look Different
## to Cyclists

When friends who normally do their commuting by car give me directions to places in the city we share – Newcastle, Australia – they may as well be speaking in Russian. They speak as though I should know the names of what they call 'main roads' and the landmarks along them. I'm afraid they're deluded. Theirs is a version of our city I had barely gotten to know when I defected to cycling two decades ago.

My city, the city mapped in my bicyclist's mind, is a network of paths following the course of storm water canals, quiet backstreets, some decaying industrial zones, bushland and parks and disused rail corridors – some of those now converted for bicycle use, making them 'rail-trails' in the parlance of bicycling advocacy. My main roads are those hidden routes I refer to. My landmarks are gaps in fences, culverts cutting underneath rail lines and roads and paths and bridges that long ago slipped from anyone's maintenance schedules.

A central idea of this book is that each cyclist develops a similar cycle-space map of their city in their bicycling mind. Much about these maps depends on individuals' perceptions, subcultures and the way codes of behaviour change from city to city. It is in deference to the last of these variables that I begin each chapter with a portrait of a particular city, based on my experience cycling around it. I believe being alive to this idea of cycle space and understanding the various motivations behind cycling can help architects and urban designers redeem the post-industrial city.

## Political Climates and
## Dutch Standards

Until a decade ago we might have said the Dutch overreacted to the oil crisis of the 1970s by taking street space from driving to make space for cycling. In countries like mine, Australia, we just rationed our petrol, tightened our belts, shot films like *Mad Max*, weathered the storm and then went back to driving.

In one sense, Australian leaders of my parents' generation did the right thing. Oil production resumed. Urban populations found space for freeways and parking by continuing to relocate from cities to suburbs. Most importantly, people proved willing to pay.

Not all of us, though, acquiesce willingly. Year by year, more of us are feeling as though we've been duped; and in larger cities like New York, Sydney, Paris and London, so many are seeing the folly of driving – in particular the cost for parking – that conditions today favour pro-cycling mayors.

Yet even those mayors who have been elected on bike transport platforms are making slow progress when you compare their results to rates of cycling taken for granted in the Netherlands. A Dutch city needs to have a bike modal share of 40 or 50 percent before it stands out as especially bike friendly. A tenth as much cycling makes Portland America's star.

It is not for a lack of driver or rider awareness campaigns, city bike schemes, rider training or critical mass demonstrations that young cycling cities can't hold a candle to cities in the Netherlands. In the industrialized world it is the places with continuous bike paths, segregated from traffic, that have high rates of bicycle transport. The Dutch have the best bike infrastructure and the most people on bikes; the Danes have slightly fewer bike paths and slightly less cycling; and so on down the rankings until we reach countries like the USA and Australia, with virtually no bike paths and around 1 per cent of all trips made by bike. So, if Dutch infrastructure is the recipe for high rates of cycling, why hasn't London, for instance, just built it? It only took the Dutch a few years in the late 1970s to substantially reconfigure their streets to protect cyclists from cars and opening car doors. Why is it taking the others so long? Why are affluent cities like New York, Sydney and Paris – all with pro-cycling mayors – struggling to achieve bike modal shares that the Dutch wouldn't even know how to measure?

Pro-bike politicians in non-cycling nations face a dilemma that did not face Dutch politicians back in the 1970s. Leaders in countries like mine represent voters who weren't alive last time cycling was mainstream, in the 1940s and early 1950s. Such constituencies would sooner bring the Mandatory Vegetarianism Party to power than an administration promising to reduce space for driving and parking for the sake of something so hard to imagine as mass bicycle transport. By contrast, voters in the Netherlands in the late 1970s had a fresh memory of interwar cycling, barely affected by private car ownership. Moreover, most were still regular cyclists

themselves. In the minds of Dutch voters there has never been a time since bikes were invented when they weren't more important than cars.

This book presents an architectural solution to the other politicians' dilemma. Most cities have redundant rail routes, high-lines and even underground spaces that architects have already been helping convert into green space with obligatory bike paths. Cities also have concrete-lined waterways waiting to be naturalized, and in the process activated with bike paths. Most cities have former industrial sites, docklands and contaminated brownfields with space for bike paths and, vitally, space for the private development that will fund all the bike paths I am proposing.

Taken together, the kinds of sites mentioned provide scope for a sparse lattice of Dutch urbanism – complete with new housing – in the negative space left by old industries. It is space car-loving voters have not been contesting because the city to which they are attached turns its back on brownfields and waterways. Cyclists, meanwhile, know this space well, having been using it to avoid cars.

The significance of this book, at this time, is that it offers a third way to enable bicycle transport, one that doesn't put cycling into conflict with driving. Behind the chapters to follow is the idea that newly redeveloped pockets of cities, connected by greenways, will provide a broad lattice for those who would like to orient their lives around active transport, while other parts of our cities are left as they are: more or less dependent on cars.

The design strategies and theoretical primers contained in this book go as naturally with brownfield renewal projects and greenways as drive-through fast food joints go hand-in-hand with sprawl and arterial roads. That is not to say the architectural principles of zones that favour cycling can't work in car-dependent parts of the city. There can be slippage, just as car parks can be built to serve bike trails, or as cyclists can take their bikes through the carwash. What we can't have are false expectations that cycling can thrive on what has been claimed as car drivers' turf. In countries where cycling has been marginalized, it is more likely to thrive at the margins.

Bold cantilever of Harvard Graduate School of Design nicely shelters bike parking, Cambridge, MA
Photo: Steven Fleming

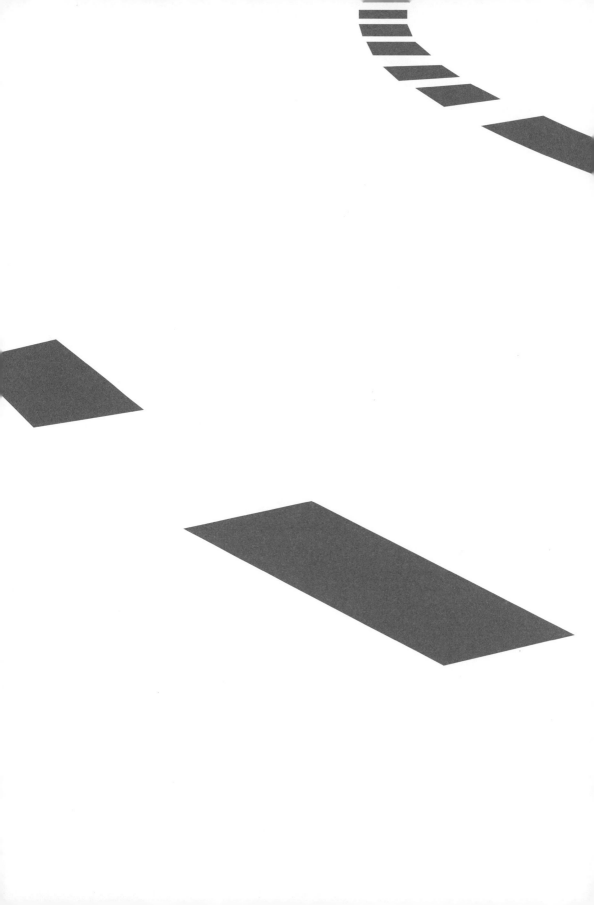

# Cycle

# Because

# It's

# PRACTICAL

# Amsterdam

Traffic engineers never quite got the foothold in Amsterdam that they would have liked to. You can sense their dismay: land cut into strips by canals, a high water table and silty soils, and not least a population who had already taken to bikes the way mice take to treadmills. What was it with the Dutch that they found cycling more appealing than the cosy warmth offered by cars?

Putting it down to their country being flat would be trite. Many countries have flat regions into which this tiny nation could be fit many times over. If terrain alone led to cycling, the century-long obsession in Amsterdam with bikes would be mirrored in other flat cities, for example Chicago. Perhaps we can accredit it to the high water table that has ruled out basement car parking. People in Amsterdam only use bikes because they have no place to park anything else. Although, if that were the sole reason, I suspect more Dutch would ride eBikes – electronically assisted bicycles that have the extra advantages of a car, without taking up the additional space. These, however, occupy a relatively small market share in the Netherlands. It is often said that Amsterdam's population density explains all the cycling. People have less distance to travel. However, that argument loses strength, too, when we look at the high rates of cycling between regional towns dotted all over the Netherlands. Bike trips, in these parts of the country, can easily be as long as average car trips in sprawling automobile-dependent cities in other parts of the world. Neither does the density argument account for low rates in cycling in other dense cities, for example New York, where less than half of 1 per cent of all trips are taken by bike. Finally, the weather can also be ruled out as a causal factor as no one would argue that the people of Amsterdam enjoy the world's most conducive conditions for cycling. Dutch weather is plainly atrocious! The only thing that does uniquely connect

the people of Amsterdam to their tradition of cycling is that, in the seventeenth century, their city was the principal stronghold of Calvinism.

John Calvin's doctrine of predestination may seem an odd thing to mention in a book about cycling, but it does seem key to why the Dutch cycle so much. Calvin was of the harsh view that each of our souls is predestined for Heaven or Hell. Calvinist Christians didn't live disciplined and austere lives in the hope they might improve their chances of salvation. Doing it tough was a matter of ascertaining one's fate, of being satisfied in one's self, that you were wheat and not chaff. Though the bicycle arrived 300 years later than Calvinism (as hard as that it is to believe given the ancient look of some bikes here), enough stoic pride remained in the national psyche that the bike was picked up like the Bible.

Where mechanisms of status in the USA meant anyone could be a nobleman, so long as he drove a Cadillac, counting oneself among the Netherlands's elite requires cycling to work in all weather. The numbers of people going to church might have gone through the floor in recent decades, but that hasn't put a stop to the Calvinist flavour embodied in Dutch cycling.

The same can be said of buildings designed to support cycling in the Netherlands. Compared to American ones, Dutch

pages 12 - 13
Cycling in Amsterdam
Photos: Mikael
Colville-Andersen

buildings for bikes look like Reformed churches, as compared to churches of the Baroque. The exaggerated style of Baroque building during the Counter-Reformation was intended to woo people back to the Catholic Church. In the same fashion it seems Americans today are building flamboyant curvilinear bicycle stations as a means to woo the population back from cars to cycling. However, in Amsterdam, the architecture being built to support cycling is not for those who need signs to see. It is for the elect.

Their Calvinist ancestors hated the thought that they might be counted among the heathen unwashed. Today high culture serves a role like the one that was once played by God.

No Dutchman wants anyone to think he is culturally illiterate. So when the Russian artist duet Komar & Melamid phone polled 1,000 residences of the Netherlands, and asked questions to determine what the statistically average Dutchman most wants in a painting, they learned it would be a non-representational work, something resembling abstract expressionism. In comparison, an earlier survey found that what the

statistically average American most wants in a painting is a landscape, complete with a deer and George Washington.

The beauty of Dutch architecture, which voters support with policies guaranteeing a vibrant architectural culture, is likewise not for the unwashed to behold. If MVRDV's Dutch Pavilion is at all characteristic of this nation's tastes, then it is for works lesser mortals find ugly. Dutch architecture exists to please those willing to seek explanations, of the kind people seek in abstract expressionism.

Another way Calvinists convinced themselves that they were of God's chosen was by their frugality. In the age of cycling, that means bikes so old and so worthless you can afford to leave one at every train station you are every likely to go to. Audit a Dutchman's keys, and at least one will belong to a bike he has abandoned – not that this was ever his conscious intention. Ask, and he'll tell you he means to go back and retrieve it. Given the bicycle parking station outside Amsterdam Centraal is almost as full overnight as it is through the day, it would be fair to guess that keys to half of those locks are jingling in pockets all over the country.

The building wouldn't be needed if the problem of abandoned bikes were simply managed. Which raises the question of why the city built it at all? I prefer to bypass the official statement (of it being a temporary structure, etcetera) and bring it all back to John Calvin: saintliness shines brightest against a dark backdrop. Women openly selling their bodies on Oudezijds Voorburgwal, marijuana cafes, bestiality tapes and towers of bikes abandoned by sinners – it's all just a foil. A way for the sheep to distinguish themselves from the goats.

# Chapter 1

# Why Stroll When You Can Roll?

### Pipe Dreams of
### Walkable Cities

Rust destroyed our family car in eight years. Had we put into managed funds all that we paid to buy the darned thing, have it registered and insured, serviced, fixed, fuelled, parked, etcetera, I have calculated we would be 120,000 Australian dollars richer right now. Bless the day I took that contraption off to the auction, and bought a Dutch *bakfiets* instead.

The Dutch are such practical people. They make bikes in plain colours, without point-of-sale gimmicks, that are easier to ride than walking with groceries, despite how ungainly they look. I can load this cargo bike with shopping bags and kids and make it home with laughable ease. I have heard people say: 'That must be hard to steer,' scratching their heads, having not yet understood what the push-rod is doing. I tell them: 'Not really,' and hold up the apple I'm eating with my left hand.

Most of what is worth reading on the subject of practical cycling first appeared in the Dutch language. As well as inventing bikes to cart kids and food, they have written the book on protected bike lanes, bike parking in and around buildings and the best way to augment a rail network with short-distance cycling.

The down-side to cycling being practical and commonplace is the lack of occasion surrounding it. There seems little point in owning a dream bike, or wearing cycling-specific attire, or even just taking a bucket and sponge to your bike in the Netherlands. Sure, there are bike scenes, enthusiasts and some events, but overwhelmingly Dutch cycling does not invite celebration.

You celebrate cycling in countries like mine, where city streets make cycling so hard that finding any safe haven is a cause for collective outpourings of joy. As cyclists we're concentrated in particular areas, which planners never envisioned would be quite so bike-laden. We get there and want to rip off our helmets, admire one another's equipment and make weaving patterns like dolphins. Cycling here is edifying, in ways the Dutch seem unwilling to humour.

Let us not forget, though, that city planners didn't set out to make spaces for pure cycling pleasure in non-cycling nations. In architecture books before this one, cycling has always come second to walking. Space for bikes happened by accident. Like any accident, the one that created all of this cycle space involved two things in motion, each unaware of the other, until they collided. The first was the will to build walkable cities.

By degrees and through the agency of theorists like Aldo Rossi, Collin Rowe, Jan Gehl, Gordon Cullen, Leon Krier and many others, the European city was emerging as an article of faith in the planning community. It was no hindrance that European old towns, as models, caught the public imagination in ways functionalist theory had dismally failed to. By the mid-1980s, professionals were referring to gateways, axes and nodes, uniform datums formed by neighbouring parapets, dense figure-ground plans, fine-grain permeable edges, and so forth, all with the end goal of making cities convivial places to walk.

It is as though the new world had just come back from a weekend in the old one – or Venice, to be precise – rejuvenated by their time not encum-

1
The weight control benefits of cycling over walking are borne out by a recent Harvard study, that found: 'Women who bicycled more than 4 h/wk had lower odds of gaining weight compared with those [brisk walkers] who reported no bicycling.' Diane Feskanich, Anne Lusk, Rania Mekary and Walter Willett, 'Bicycle Riding, Walking, and Weight Gain in Premenopausal Women', *Archives of Internal Medicine*, vol. 170 (2010) no. 12, 1050-1056.

bered by cars. They got off their planes with the medieval town fresh in their minds, ready to project it upon the shitty dumps they called home. 'Walkability' would be a panacea for every urban ailment, from sprawl, to the sterility of modernism, to their ill health, to their loneliness.

And, just at that time when imaginers were re-imagining urbanism, a second phenomenon went into motion: space in the city was becoming available for planners to test their hypotheses. The will to build walkable cities collided with the opportunity to reclaim former wharves and turn them into café strips, to make parks and new condos where previously there had been rail handling yards right in the middle of town, or to convert warehouses into office suites and apartments. Early schemes like London's Isle of Dogs (former docklands), Paris's Park de la Villette (once a slaughter yard) and Chicago's Millennium Park (built over rail lines) satiated architecture magazines' hunger for more than just renovations and infill to splash on their covers. Indeed a large chunk of the buildings and public art schemes that architects have drooled over in glossies for the past 20 years are associated with cities entering their post-industrial phase.

What a boon for the *flâneur*, to have all these level sites neatly paved for dining alfresco, decontaminated for planting tall palms, flooded with mini lakes in which he might see his reflection, zoned mixed-use so that there may be shops for him to stroll by, and all of it touched by architects with highly developed picturesque sensibilities. What top spots for our *flâneur* to stroll hand in hand with his sweetheart! For him, maybe. I lack the patience.

I can hear planners referring to all of those alfresco cafés as anchors, to drag me on over to some otherwise lifeless point on a paddock. The trees look as lonely as Giacomettis; no one dared plant them in forests: muggers might hide there! The retail outlets are mostly empty for lease. The Claus Oldenburg sculpture lost my interest before I read the plaque and learned it was not by Claus Oldenburg. And if that lake there, way over yonder, is beckoning me to come hither, I might just throw myself in it and drown.

I confess, that's a hyperbolic portrayal, but I suspect you too have walked around one of these 'renewed' brownfields and wondered why all the hype. They're nothing like Venice. They have little intrigue for the pedestrian. No narrow streets or dark alleys. No masses crammed into tiny dwellings spilling into piazzas. They have nothing to delight people on foot, unless those people enjoy feeling lonely.

I could add a paragraph here on what might have gone wrong, but as a keen cyclist, it doesn't really concern me that the walkable cities of old could not be replicated. If the pension funds financing much of this urban renewal would rather build malls than corner stores, and apartment blocks instead of small walk-ups and infill developments, let that be as it is; because, as a cyclist, I find joy in the city resulting.

By reading this book, you're indulging my bike-centric worldview that says walking is tiresome and boring. For starters, walking wears the heels of men's shoes, and snaps those of ladies. It makes us look like drivers who have just been let out for air – at least that's what people strolling look like to me. Compared to cycling, regular walking hardly helps manage weight gain.[1] And most painful of all, for me, is how walking makes me feel as though I am still eight, waiting for Santa to bring me a bike.

Pedestrians too look at cyclists with envy. How could they not, especially when they see us in these revamped former industrial parts of our cities that are so inviting of cycling! Too vast to be pleasant for walking, and much smaller in scale than places designed around car use – such as Las Vegas – these places, which are cropping up wherever industry has been vacating, are of an in-between scale. A bicycling scale. It can even be said that much of the new architecture spawned by such places is ideally viewed from the arcing, leaning, moving point of view of a cyclist – a thought I will expand upon later.

### The Big Picture of
### Brownfield Urban Renewal

The most important thing to understand about cities that grew around industry is this: they grew around industry. The industrialists who procured land for factories, who built the wharves and who chose the course of the railway lines built *their* networks first. Commercial, civic and residential areas just fell in around them. That is why non-industrial networks can seem so fragmented, with neighbourhoods on the wrong sides of the tracks, the shady sides of the ridges, on the wrong banks of rivers, downwind from factory smokestacks, sometimes just seeming like unfortunate series of afterthoughts. The rail easement your city now turns its back on, could have been its first act of cultivation. In planned capital cities, like Washington, DC in the USA, or Canberra in Australia, the first planning gesture (the Mall or Grand Boulevard) continues to occupy centre stage. But in former industrial cities, the routes that came first have been eclipsed in many people's minds by the roads that came later. The original routes are like forgotten wax lines on paper, doing little now aside from annoying all those who would like to paint the car city.

Networks of canals and railway lines, which once stood out from fields, have become so deeply buried underneath networks of roads that architects are able to forget it was these that linked industrial sites to each other. They ask how a particular brownfield site might mesh with road networks, which may only date to the 1940s or 1950s, when deciding the best location for their camouflaged car park. They look for light rail hubs, belonging to the youngest networks of all, when deciding where to build pedestrian flyovers. While water edges, canals and old rail lines are commonly taken as routes for recreational walking and cycling, they are overlooked as feeders of large numbers of people. Architects can't imagine greenways or promenades providing their commercial developments with the volumes of people they will need to succeed.

If they would only imagine a day when all these neighbouring industrial sites have been redeveloped with the obligatory non-vehicular promenade of each sewn into the next, they then might see how networks of docklands, shunting yards, landfills, mills, old rail lines and the edges of creeks, rivers and harbours are being transformed into vast networks of bike paths – at least in the eyes of people with bikes, and limited other safe places for riding. As a cyclist, I see parallel cities coming into focus, on industrial land, with their backs turned on those places where people drive. I see alter-cit-

<u>top & middle right</u>
The Shweeb, New Zealand
Courtesy of Peter Cossey,
Shweeb

<u>left</u>
The Orange Cube, by architects Jakob + Macfarlane,
exemplifies a style of
architecture common to
urban renewal zones that
rewards cyclists more
than pedestrians, Lyon.
(Author Steven Fleming in
foreground).
Photo: Gabriella Sanderson

<u>bottom</u>
Staff member riding her
bike inside Frankfurt
Airport
Photo: Steven Fleming

ies more suited to bike use than walking or driving, or even light rail, buses and ferries.

These areas will not need buried car parking stations. They might not even need much public transport. Virtually every trip taken to them, and within them, could be by bicycle; and people's health and wellbeing would be vastly improved as a result. Apartment buildings could have spiralling bike ramps, rather than elevators or stairs. We could ride inside shopping malls, the way staff ride inside Frankfurt Airport. Wind assisted, fully enclosed bicycle expressways could be the new metros: more fun, more healthy and with no waiting for trains or modal changes. We would see parallel bike routes: some for slow fashionable cyclists, in public places where slow cyclists can go to be seen; some for mountain bike riders, weaving between trees to emulate trails; others made especially for 12-year-old boys, with whoopdeedo jumps, because kids, well, like to jump. I'm imagining the vacuum left as industry moves out of cities, being filled by a kind of urban environment, where it is assumed people will ride bikes, as surely as they wear shoes. Look at birds: whether moving between continents or just from one limb on a tree to the next, they use their wings. Bikes can be our wings.

I know this can't happen in every city, and I know that what I am proposing comes on the back of lost industrial activity within the cities where it is possible. It wasn't me, though, who pushed the docks to deeper waters and the factories to China; and it wasn't me who replaced them with urban environments too vast for walking. Neither did I say individual projects should all be huge and alienating to people on foot. But they are, and look set to only get bigger. They are so big in scale because financiers – pension funds mainly – don't muck around. Scale equals profit. But while I didn't make the new city, I am able to find something good in it. Like a hermit crab stumbling upon just the right shell, the city can be redeemed, made healthy, humane and worth waking up to, if we just see its real potential. Its potential for cycling.

### Cycle Space in Your Mind, in My Mind and in Our Minds

Often I will be returning to the subject of redeveloped industrial land. It has such a key role to play in the proliferation and diversification of cycling that it warrants a lion's share of attention. However, let's not make 'cycle space' a cipher for 'brownfield'. Cycle space is the organizing system an individual cyclist projects upon his or her city, in the sense that airspace is an imaginary system used to make sense of the sky. This analogy will keep us on track.

It is an analogy too, that brings clarity to a salient characteristic of cycle space: how it is plural, with loci residing in each of our minds. Airspace is defined by aviation authorities. Flying is too dangerous for that to be otherwise. But using a bike to get places is hardly more dangerous than walking. Authorities generally don't care where people ride – except for in flashpoint centres of conflict, such as New York with its embarrassing and pointless bicycling crackdowns. I wonder if it is because no other country has been so uptight in the way they view cycling, that to date only America has worked with Google to map each city's officially sanctioned places for cycling on their Google maps bicycling layer?

Yet in spite of their foolish bureaucracies, few American cyclists care in the slightest where officials would legislate that they ride. They find their own way around, treat stop signs as mere suggestions to yield and ride wherever police don't physically make them dismount. Bicycle-born citizens of the world's premier motoring nation, America, make cycle space for themselves, just as cyclists do everywhere else.

My son's cycle-space map is like mine when I was his age, just a few footpaths in our local neighbourhood (or so he tells me). I have friends in the bike racing fraternity who see the entire road network as their domain, and would never stoop to use bike paths: those are for 'non-serious' cyclists, my macho mates say. But those 'non-serious' cyclists can be mighty earnest indeed when it comes to those bike paths, lobbying for more to be built and using networks of bike paths as the backbones of cycle space as they perceive it. There are mountain bike enthusiasts whose maps of cycle space are overwhelmingly concerned with nature reserves. Kids into freestyle BMX know every skate park and how to get there, with their knees kicking their chins.

Even in the Netherlands and Denmark, where theoretically bicycling infrastructure should magically appear wherever one points their nose, some cyclists shun officially sanctioned routes that don't suit their mood. I rode the coastal route north from Copenhagen through Vedbæk, and encountered far more cyclists on the vehicular road, where there wasn't a shoulder, than I saw on the protected bicycle route flanking the train line. The reason was obvious. The road heading north from Copenhagen is more picturesque, following the edge of the sea. Cycle space, or cycle spaces, cannot be dictated. They are individual constructs in each of our minds.

Like many competitive cyclists, my training regime sees me spending a few hours each week cycling in cyberspace. I have a spare road bike perma-nently mounted in a frame in my bedroom, made by the Dutch Virtual Reality Cycling company Tacx. It seems fitting that sports cyclists from such a boring flat country as the Netherlands would have conceived this device, which takes me out of my bedroom to virtual islands with moun-tains and rolling hills. Tacx users, who could be anywhere in the world, meet in these realms to race in real time. We steer and overcome resistance provided by our motor brakes, which accurately simulate the effects of gradients, road surfaces, winds and the slipstreams made by each others' avatars. As I'm writing, my real legs are really aching from a ride I took moments ago, in a synthetic realm I know as intimately as my bike route to work. If we speak of cycle space in a way that can accommodate something as peculiar as this, we will have succeeded.

### Public Infrastructure for Individual Motion

Calling cycle space a personal thing, for each of us to define in our own way, brings clarity to one of the major frustrations facing designers of bicycling infrastructure; a frustration they can't wish away. Bicycle transit is lightweight, nimble, individualistic and therefore always erring towards chaos. The same can't be said of transit modes involving less agile machines, certainly not trains, and not really cars either. We remark most on drivers' careless lapses, but ignore what Reyner Banham described as their 'acquiescence in an incredibly demanding man/machine system'.[2] Commensurate with their right to wield armoured, weather protected, load carrying, lockable, heavy machinery around city streets, drivers accept a whole raft of responsibilities cyclists should naturally be entitled to shirk; the obligation to be proficiency tested, for instance.

Given the featherweight force (force equalling weight times velocity) that a cyclist can bring to a collision, we can tolerate cyclists riding one handed, suddenly stopping, or exploiting their agility to turn on a dime. It is slightly harder to accept couples blocking bike lanes as they ride hand-in-hand at lovers' pace, or scoff-laws running red lights, or fast riders brushing by slow ones at triple their speed. However, lest cycling rates stagnate while pluralism takes greater hold, infrastructure designers need to be alive to the immergence of bicycling subcultures and a wide range of riding styles. Bikes aren't as unpredictable as pogo sticks, although that comparison is more useful than expecting bikes to behave in the cumbersomely uniform manner of cars. As true as it is that all cars are similar, it is true that all cyclists are more or less different.

In the urban centres of the Netherlands and Denmark, roughly a third of all trips are made using bicycles. Many see the glass as half full (okay, one-third full), and start thinking they have found the ideal way for everyone to cycle in cities. Riding upright, not wearing helmets, riding in heels, owning some old thing granny left in her will, and any other hackneyed cliché we might distil from reality, soon become dogmas to be taken and preached to the non-cycling world, as though the Dutch and Danish rates of bicycle transit can only be matched if we parody their bicycling heritage.

I am more critical. I see all the trips Dutch and Danish folk make by means other than cycling, and am forced to conclude that, as cycling nations, neither is fully realized. Think of it this way: if a country used cars for less than one third of all urban trips, and far less than that for regional ones, would we call it a nation of drivers? Around two thirds of all trips, in each of those countries, are still made by car, bus or train. Both nations are reaping less than a third of the potential public health dividends that cycling could win them, only a third of the added prosperity, a third of the emissions reductions and only a third of the additional leisure time that comes when people see bicycle commuting as leisure time. No nation can claim bikes have delivered all of the externalities – both economic and quality-of-life – that they potentially can.

Neither are postcard portrayals of Nordic blondes on upright bikes truly representative of bicycle transport in either country. Postcards don't show young lads tearing up bike paths on motorized scooters, especially in the Netherlands. The thousands of Lycra clad riders of road racing bikes, who also get counted in bike share reports, aren't so exotic, and so they escape the world's gaze. Propaganda images portraying a gentler more ecologically friendly lifestyle don't show the chain smoking hipsters on track bikes, or bearded middle-aged dudes weaving dirt tracks into their regular com-

2
Reyner Banham, *Los Angeles: The Architecture of Four Ecologies* (Berkeley: The University of California Press, 2001), 195-196, 199-201, 202-204. Originally published in 1971.

3
An article in the online magazine *Bike Hub*, 'When designing infrastructure for new cyclists, ignore the existing ones, says study', shows how cyclists are offended when their knowledge and experience looks like it might be dismissed. Available HTTP: http://www.bikehub.co.uk/news/sustainability/when-designing-for-new-cyclists-ignore-the-existing-ones-says-study/ (accessed 11 September 2011).

mutes on their mountain bikes, or highways stretched from Belgium to Sweden, all teeming with cars. Photos aren't spread on the web of bikes with thin, high-pressure tires, which are almost as prevalent in Copenhagen as the classic bikes.

In the short term, exporting clichés from these countries will no doubt help diversify cycling in places where bicycles have only been seen as sporting equipment, or toys. Long term, though, subscribers to all of the cycling world's orthodoxies (slow cycling, mounting biking, road racing, ad so forth) will have to accept that their particular denomination was not the only one admitted to bicycling heaven.

## Growing Pluralism
## as Cycling Rates Rise

Cycling advocacy groups like the League of American Bicyclists (formerly Wheelmen) and long-term cycling journalists are understandably inclined to defend their expert positions against 'non-expert' advice – meaning advice from anyone who has not ridden thousands of miles on their bikes, the way they do. Woe to Professor Colin Pooley of the Lancaster Environment Centre for suggesting existing cyclists' views be taken with a grain of salt, when planning to recruit new cyclists from populations of regular drivers.[3] Creative new proposals for the built environment – of the kind architects and urban planners would table if they turned their minds to making bicycling mainstream – are likely to be viewed as ideas from Mars by experts invested in their knowledge of how things have been.

Dear American Wheelmen, before you throw my book on the fire, imagine for a moment some distant Utopia, where the ratio of bikes to cars is a neat inversion of the usual equation: instead of almost everyone moving by car, almost everyone will be moving by bike. In built environments where all the barriers are gone that currently prevent people from across the whole social spectrum from cycling, cycling will be diverse in ways you are not prepared to imagine.

While narrow visions of what cycling can be, and can't be, have undoubtedly contributed to the failure of bicycle transport in the USA, no place is immune from homogenous thinking. The percentage of trips made by bike in Copenhagen seems to have stalled in the past decade at just below 40 per cent. Of the remaining 60 per cent of people being transported, there would be some who can't cycle, for whatever reason, but there would also be people whose cycling style is not catered for by the city's one-size-fits-all planning approach. They might have too far to go to be shepherded along at just 20 km p/h by traffic lights timed to favour the mean. Slower, less skilful riders might find it stressful when herds overtake them on 2.4-m-wide bike paths. Then come the hipsters on their fixed gear bikes with no brakes, looking for the smallest gaps to squeeze through, though really wishing they were allowed to squeeze between trucks and busses. Denmark produced the world's first commercially available velomobile (pedal powered car), the Leitra, but its bike paths makes these hard to use. Add the Christiania cargo bikes and child cyclists, and it is easy to see why cyclists in Copenhagen are now more frightened of one another than cars.

My sense is that Copenhagen will need to give the whole of many roads over to cycling, and engineer these for multiple speeds, before the bike share breaks past 40 per cent. Until then, Copenhagen will fall well short of the Utopia I'm asking America's wheelmen to kindly imagine.

Another, even more exciting, picture emerges if we sharpen our focus and look, with a little imagination, at cities within cities, where the bike share really is close to 100 per cent. Can the Manhattan Waterfront Greenway be considered a city in isolation? Not quite, but almost. If the piers along the Hudson were shut off to cars, then topped with residential and office towers designed to accommodate cyclists, the Manhattan Waterfront Greenway could be looked upon as the beginnings of a long, thin city of cyclists. In ancient times Athens was an elongated, dumbbell-shaped city, designed to keep non-Athenians out of Piraeus Harbour, the Acropolis area and the walled-off road in between. Look, if you will, at the western edge of Manhattan as a protected city like ancient Athens. Imagine a roof over the bike path and suddenly 100 per cent of people living within a city (albeit a city *within* a city) are cycling.

Scenarios like this are poised to play out wherever waterfront greenways, rail trails or other politically expedient routes to lay bike paths have the potential of linking brownfield sites currently earmarked for urban renewal. When I think of the opportunities for cycling as urban renewal sites start joining hands – waterfronts and rail easements their outstretched arms – I know cycle space needs a diffuse ontology. We will have these cities within cities where cycling isn't impeded, meaning no particular demographic or bike tribe has a chance to define it. Just as cities built to make driving mainstream happily accommodated everything from Ferraris to VW buses painted with peace signs, these cities within cities, where cycling can flourish, will make the horizontal rivalries between today's bicycling tribes seem laughable in retrospect.

As well as pilots of velomobiles, riders of tall-bikes and downhill mountain bike daredevils, there might be patrons of pedal-powered monorail systems, such as the *Shweeb*, bicycling counterparts to drivers of lavish cars, lovers of bling-laden low-rider dragsters, people who would fit sails to recumbent bicycles, hipsters with attitude, stunt riders on trials bikes and thousands of others none of us can possibly think of while cycling rates are as low as they presently are. We can expect cycling to become exponentially more diverse as its modal share pushes beyond merely one-third, and for it to attain infinite diversity in the event that 100 per cent of all transportation became human powered.

If we allow our thinking about bicycle transportation to be shaped by ways we have had to think about cars – because they're so dangerous – the potential chaos of a hyper-bike city will be too frightening to even consider. We could allay our fears quickly and simply though, with a trip to a skate park. See how kids can traverse a field of grind rails, concrete volcanoes and quarter pipes with others crossing their paths on their stunt bikes, scooters and skateboards. They miss each other as surely as rush hour crowds in Grand Central Station, or as Amsterdam's cyclists at corners: a swarm hits a swarm and none place a foot down. Each just wriggles on through.

Only when it has been locked into our thinking that diversity is a positive aim can we tentatively begin to discuss types of cycle space that most can agree on. Now I am referring to those routes in all cities that are familiar to most who ride bikes, regardless of riding styles. Green corridors are the most obvious examples. Their users include people who ride to save time, to save money, to save losing their bike race this coming weekend, to save the planet, to save their hearts, to save being bored sitting at home doing nothing, or to save looking uncool now that cycling has become chic. Even though I am saying cycle space is a personal construct, I know I am speaking on behalf of most of these cyclists when I say green corridors can be categorized as belonging to their cycle-space maps of their cities.

## Shared Cycle Space

Cycle space, in my life, in my city, still comprises many insalubrious places. My bicycling-mind's map of my city includes underpasses smelling of urine, road crossings that I am sure the traffic engineers designed with the intension of killing me, and some rather barren stretches of bike path alongside storm-water canals. I call all of this cycle space, but admit that much of it is depressing.

The former industrial zones of my city are those I thank for the expansion of my cycle-space map to include places that edify: green corridors, waterfront promenades, the curtilage around warehouse conversions with all of their character, gravel paths winding through former wastelands that have now become parklands. I can imagine a future when my whole life falls within spaces where my father and grandfathers had to drag themselves off to for work. My home, office, shops, kids' schools and anywhere I might recreate will be on soil my ancestors only knew when it was black, in zones they only knew as places to trudge in their work clothes.

In writing this book, I am hoping planners and architects redeveloping former industrial tracts see trudging as the eternal curse on this land. Remodelling it with walking in mind would have been a laughable thought to our grandparents. To me, it still is.

In the last year or two I have noticed an increase in numbers of cyclists, compared to pedestrians, on my city's harbour-side promenade. There isn't much parking, and people here have that aversion to buses and trains that is common in car dependent societies. So young people and families are coming, all the way from their homes, on their bikes. Each of them is enlivening the public realm, as they would have done as pedestrians; only instead of boredom, frustration and a feeling of being dwarfed by big buildings, they are rewarded with a commanding, aesthetic experience. The buildings, core-ten steel public works of art, spitting fountains, museums and predictable attractions like these, pass by them at roughly the speed shop fronts would pass them in old parts of town, if they were walking. Bringing their bikes redeems their experience of an over-scaled urban environment.

A bike rickshaw business has started here, to cater for those who persist with driving, then parking, then trudging. Purely for research purposes, I presented to their headquarters as though I could be any other backpack-

top
Monthly critical mass
ride, San Francisco
Photo: Steven Fleming

middle left
Pictograms near the
World Trade Center
site, New York, NY
Photo: Mikael
Colville-Andersen

middle right
Pedicab service, Paris
Photo: Mikael
Colville-Andersen

bottom
Behind the apparent
chaos of cycling in
Amsterdam, subtleties
are at play that mean
cyclists rarely collide.
Photo: Mikael
Colville-Andersen

er or student, and hired a bike, to try my luck making more back in fares. I spent a summer of Saturday nights cruising the promenade scooping up weary walkers stranded mid-way between restaurants and bars. Most being drunk, they yell things like 'Suckers!' at anyone walking. Other people on bikes would be glancing at me, the guy riding, with knowing smiles. It can't be too long before all the suckers catch on, and use their own bikes for bar hopping, which is when the bicycle rickshaw racket will probably end.

A great cycling city shouldn't need rickshaws. People would have their own wheels from the moment they left their homes. They would go window-shopping at 10-20 km/h. Anywhere a woman might take her handbag, I imagine she will take her bike too. We could pedal our way through the levels of buildings, which all might have ramps. Cyclists could be directed with signs, while drivers would be the ones who are made to fumble with maps – a reversal of the situation at present. If I lived someplace cold, I would be witnessing snow being ploughed from the bike tracks and onto the roads. Then I start imagining bike routes that are weather protected, with solar powered fans ensuring we never know headwinds.

For those of us who have already been organizing our lives around bike routes, pieces of that Utopian vision are in hand now. I have a bike room on the ground floor of my house. Many cyclists have that. Architects Jennifer Marsicek and Jason Roberts upstage us all: when altering their Portland, Oregon home, they added a bicycle garage, with a bicycle-width roller door on a remote so they can ride on in when it's raining. I live where I live, and work where I work, because I saw both locations were well connected in my cycle-space mind: by the docklands of my city that have been redeveloped with bars and a marina, and by the continuous promenade on which I can ride in relative bliss. I declined the offer of a larger office in the building I work in, because the small ground floor office that came with my initial appointment allows me to ride all the way to my desk. I park my bike in my office, where I keep half my wardrobe and an ironing board too. I have organized my life according to cycle space. Because of that, I see cycle space everywhere. I'm like a pilot, when he looks at the sky.

## Where Bicycle Transport Is Effectively Outlawed

As a manly pursuit, effective or 'vehicular' cycling – just like John Forester taught me to do with his book – was once, for me, a great source of pride. I asserted my right to the road. I dazzled kids in the back seats of their parents' cars. They would wave at the cyclist keeping pace with the traffic. Then I grew up.

Sure, when I have no better option, I will risk my life among trucks and cars, but if given the choice I would rather ride on a bike path flanking a river. It was the requirement to commute on rainy nights that taught me to seek alternative routes. I found at night I was safer on quiet backstreets. Seeing and hearing, up close and personal, the way cars slide in the wet had me scurrying for separate trails to avoid them completely in woolly weather. Truly atrocious conditions taught me the wisdom of ignoring dumb laws here in Australia about not riding on footpaths, if that was what was required to get home alive. Forester's thesis falls in a heap when drivers simply can't see your bike lights through the rain on their windscreens.

I suspect Forester was only ever a fair-weather cyclist, who did his riding by daylight. Just so they can boast that they ride among cars, there are vehicular cyclists who have spent their lives lobbying to have bikes put on the same legal footing as cars and to stop building bike paths. In the USA (United States of the Automobile), where not surprisingly this group receives a good hearing, the law puts bikes on the same legal footing as Hummers. Cyclists are prohibited from riding on pedestrian pathways in most American parks. Riding on sidewalks is tantamount to dropping ones trousers and defecating on them. So successfully have vehicular cyclists argued that cyclists fare better when they behave and are treated by the law as operators of vehicles that many American cities ban adolescents from riding on footpaths, even at night in the rain, when drivers have enough trouble seeing each other. Cycling for all-weather transportation, as opposed to fair-weather recreation, has been severely compromised in that country, except for where shared promenades and recreational bicycle trails can give safe all-weather cycling a foothold.

The situation in my country, Australia, in some ways is worse. Our punishment for speaking English is that buzz-phrases like 'vehicular cycling' come to us straight from the USA. Though our police aren't so vigilant with their enforcement, it is still the situation that a 13-year-old, by law, is not meant to ride on the footpath at night in the rain. Yet remarkably, most Australians don't see how laws such as these make cycling untenable. In fact, most think the opposite: that lawmakers are cyclists' best friends, because they force us all to wear helmets. Australians don't see how armour escalates danger, which escalates armour, and so on to the point where only King Arthur's knights can go riding on the street.

All-weather bicycle transport is effectively outlawed wherever *Effectively Cycling* had an influence on public policy. One can see the contrast in non-English countries. Tourists in Ravenna, in northern Italy, are provided free bikes to ride around and view mosaics. On the way they learn slow-cycling etiquette from locals, who simply ride on the footpath and along pedestrian streets when using their bikes for trips around town. The either/or debates that rage in immature cycling regions (between commuter cyclists wanting separated routes and faster cyclists guarding their right to the road) would take some explaining to the northern Italian. Why not use your own discretion to know when to ride slow on the footpath or fast on the road? Northern Italians know about both, having high rates of everyday cycling, plus a sportive cycling pedigree that predates the Lance Armstrong effect in the USA by almost a century.

It is for this reason that brownfield routes have a negligible impact on modal share rates in countries like Italy. Italians riding bikes slowly, just around town, share the same legal status as people walking, so have legal access to every footpath and pedestrian zone. The bike trail along the banks of the Tiber in Rome is one of the fastest arterial routes in that city; but in a city where any footpath, cobbled lane or piazza belongs to your cycle space, why would a neighbourhood cyclist carry their bikes down steps to the water, for the sake of a bike lane?

There are waterfront bike routes in the Netherlands too, but the bicycling life could happily go on if they were taken away. Sure, it is faster and smoother riding past the new waterfront buildings lining Amsterdam's Amstel River than battling cobbles and blind corners in the old part of town. But why seek out brownfield routes when the old town, gnarly though it may be, functions like a bicycling rink? Not surprisingly, far fewer cyclists avail themselves of the Netherlands' renewed zones with their wide-open bike routes than you will find clambering onto the Manhattan Waterfront Greenway for safety. That route in New York has made bicycle transit possible for thousands of cyclists who would otherwise have looked at the on-street routes and concluded that cycling was too tricky for them

Where safe, all weather bicycle transit has been effectively outlawed due to the underlying influence of 'vehicular cycling', we find an intense kind of cycle space, in the shadow of industry. Minneapolis, one of America's most bike friendly cities, does not have especially bike friendly streets throughout town. What they do have in Minneapolis are bicycle trails running parallel to most of the rail lines and along both banks of the Mississippi River. And what lined those riverbanks previously? Hydro powered mills, producing flour, wool, paper and cotton. In countries where traffic engineers have not given everyday cycling a chance, stretches like these make all the difference. A mass exodus of industry in a city's past can be taken as a predictor of high bicycle use later, once the job of redeveloping that land, complete with bike trails, has been completed.

And once it has given bicycle transit a foothold, land vacated by industry takes on a brilliance that inspires developers to engage high-profile architects. Many would say the High Line was the magnet for Frank Gehry's IAC headquarters and Jean Nouvel's 100 11th Avenue apartments on the lower West side of Manhattan. But the High Line is not something many locals make use of, two times a day. The cycle path on the West River is a greater amenity and arguably has been more instrumental than the High Line in flipping some of New York's attention from Broadway to the West River. BIG's West 57th Street apartment building, about to be built near the bike track, is a long way north of the High Line.

Committed cyclists (and by that I mean people who don't have backup plans to save them having to ride at night in the rain) sooner or later come to the realization that separated routes, footpaths and quiet back streets increase their chances of bicycle commuting into old age. We may own a lightweight bike with pencil thin tires that we use if we enjoy racing. We may own mountain bikes, time trialling bikes, folding bikes, track bikes, recumbent bikes, touring bikes – all kinds of bikes. To our quiver though, most of us all-weather commuters will eventually add a bike fit for that particular task, with mudguards, lights and some luggage capacity for little essentials, like our rain jackets.

I'm not mentioning equipment out of some suicidal eagerness to wade into debates about whose bike is better. Those debates are distractions that, in any case, usually just follow lines of class, age or gender. Inner-city yuppies will claim their short-reach town bikes are morally superior to suburbanites' much faster road bikes, disingenuously ignoring the greater distance people in outer suburbs may have to ride. They might not realize it, but what today is called 'cycle-chic' was first made fashionable by England's upper classes, to add a new bow to their snobbery. From *The Official Sloane Ranger Handbook*, published in 1982:

> You always bike in the same gear you wear in the office . . . helmets and goggles are for fanatics. . . . Sloan women always have large wheeled old bicycles (no idea which make) with huge wicker baskets in front. Top of the class are sit up and beg . . . bikes. . . . The bike is usually dirty, beginning to rust and in need of an oil.[4]

In like fashion, apartment dwellers will dismiss homeowners' stables of bikes as gluttonous, compared to their one Brompton or Bike Friday, kept with their boots at the door. The cycling world's older initiates will say their collections of lugged and braised bikes cannot be compared to any that are made in Taiwan. The girly girl cycling in heels on her omafiets, might roll her eyes at boys and their toys when a young guy speeds past on his fixie, but we know her choice of bike is to attract him, just as his risk taking is designed to catch her eye.

What matters in a book about buildings and cities is that everyone using pedal power is united by a need to make it home safely, when they inevitably find themselves commuting in dangerous conditions. Most tend to know the same rail trails, parks, back streets, wide footpaths and separated bike routes. Plus, in this age of urban renewal, most people committed to commuting by bike have felt the lour of former industrial zones and those protected promenades that run beside them and through them. For many, their grandfathers' former places of work will have been instrumental in their decision to become bike commuters.

Routes such as these, which most cyclists include in their cycle-space maps of their cities, have the upbeat mood of safe havens. That mood calls for architecture that represents and celebrates cycling in ways discussed in the following chapter. They are borne, though, of a practical need. Where roads and laws make most of a city hostile to cycling, riders are drawn to whatever safe routes they can find, appropriate and remake.

4
Anne Barr and Peter York, *The Official Sloane Ranger Handbook – The First Guide to What Really Matters in Life*, 10th ed. (London/Sydney: Angus & Robertson, 1982).

Cycle

Because

It's

POLITICAL

New York

Gay rights were fought for and won here. Prohibition was challenged here. The night was reclaimed here for women. It was in
New York that Jane Jacobs took on Robert Moses to save the
vitality of the West Village from expressways and order. This is
the city that takes mild discontent, gives it some clever label
and then takes it up as a cause. It is the world's agar plate of
social dilemmas. The most remarkable thing about this city is
that millions of the world's brightest sparks pay so handsomely to live here, in tiny apartments, for the honour of being able
to beam progress reports to the rest of us living out here in the
boonies, regarding the current state of those social dilemmas.

So where are things at in New York's battle for bicycle
rights? That is hard to say, but the fight does look set to go the
full 10 rounds. In the red corner, organizations like Transportation Alternatives. In the blue, the reigning defenders of public
space: American drivers.

For a user-pays city, New York does give away quite a few
freebies: free use of the toilet in Starbucks; free lunch for kids
in free public schools; free use of computers, WiFi and books
at the New York Public library; free entry into the Met
– if you choose not to pay the suggested donation. Further-
more, in a city where land is in such high demand that any
square foot could be leased in five-minute increments, no
one pays a cent for the rolling footprint of their car, or for the
braking distance ahead of their car that is off limits to anyone
else. This comes out to around 1,000 ft$^2$ (roughly 300 m$^2$) of
unavailable space in the case of a car moving at the legal
speed limit. Around SoHo, you can't rent an apartment the size
of a Winnebago for less than 8,000 dollars a month. The smart

player rents an actual Winnebago, finds roommates prepared to take turns at the wheel, and drives around SoHo 24/7. As long as their Winebago is moving, or looks as though it has just stopped to make a delivery, whatever land it is denying to others can be taken as a free gift from the city to three people choosing to live in a campervan. Free land in New York! And for what? For upholding the true values of a superpower: the consumption of oil.

page 36
Marginal space for a marginalized mode, Manhattan Bridge, New York, NY
Photo: Mikael Colville-Andersen

top
Pedestrians and opening car doors make road side cycling a stressful endeavour, New York, NY
Photo: Mikael Colville-Andersen

left
Manhattan Bridge, New York, NY
Photo: Mikael Colville-Andersen

right
The Danish designed Bullitt cargo bike in 'The Big Apple', New York, NY
Photo: Mikael Colville-Andersen

In fairness, a bicycle hoards some space as well: maybe five square feet underneath, and five ahead in its braking zone. If a car takes 300 m$^2$, and a cyclist 3 m$^2$, a pedestrian would occupy about half a square metre. So forget congestion taxes. Why not charge for public land according to use? Two cents per hour for pedestrians, ten cents per hour for cyclists and ten dollars per hour for cars? If this idea was picked up by New York's Bolshie community, they would give it some fancy label, and within weeks start stencilling price tags on public sidewalks and roads. So long as I don't get the bill for the cleanup, a stencil campaign would be great.

A lot that might be said of New York's bicycle battles has already been churned over a hundred times by that city's hyperdiligent press. It is, after all, a city of wannabe Truman Capotes, prepared to blog for nothing and write for free papers for pennies. The protected bike path along Prospect

Park West, the critical mass mass-detention of 2004, what DOT commissioner Janette Sadik-Khan had for breakfast this morning and the scandalous remarks of every right-wing shock jock have been poured over enough.

The net sum of all this debate is that an understated proportion of drivers seem to be paranoid about hitting a cyclist, for fear they will be taken to court. They see cyclists as cruising for accidents, so they steer clear. I have never been given such a wide berth on a bike as I have in New York – by most drivers anyway; there is always some guy, in some huge black machine, ready to intimidate a cyclist from behind with his engine and horn. But of course his behaviour only eggs on the cyclist to stay in his way longer, both parties secretly itching for a not-too-serious row. Each knows they can go home and report news of this encounter to a DJ or blogger, and have thousands of people take notice, because their little tiff happened at the world's epicentre.

# Chapter 2

# From Cars to Bikes

### Carchitecture and
### Bicycletecture

Back when I was studying architecture, a number of my classmates and I used to ride bikes to our lectures. We would line them up on the veranda of our Sydney modernist-style classroom and get to talking about internal cable routes, indexed gear levers and clip-in pedals – all innovations in the late 1980s. Meanwhile, our lecturers – all men, as I recall – did their bonding down at the car park, over their Peugeots, Rovers, Citroëns, Renaults and other European-made cars. In the design studio they would try to put stars in our eyes by extolling the wonders of self-levering headlights. Car design set architects a benchmark for excellence: that was the message.

When showing us slideshows of great houses, the opportunity was never missed to explain how some cantilever elegantly made space for the family car to slip in underneath. As the threat of global warming got stronger, those same slide-shows and stories made increasing references to the houses' low energy, and the better mileage on new Citroëns.

I wonder if they could have possibly chosen a paragon of design excellence that has done the world any more harm. Maybe if they tried to turn our minds towards higher ideals with photos of nicely built gallows or warplanes, shown us their favourite porn videos, or pulled out and lit big Cuban cigars. You know I'm being unfair, because you know cars were, and to a large part remain, emblems of progress, which architects have always been there to promote.

The age of the car didn't just produce new kinds of town plans, serpentine and sprawling. It produced car-specific buildings, ways for architects to think about buildings, in fact a whole raft of architectural principles that would otherwise not have come into being. Today, with the push to get commuters out of their cars and onto bikes, architectural thinking seems set to change yet again. Architects at the vanguard are turning away from the car as an emblem and source of inspiration, and are looking at bikes instead. The inevitability of cycling's ascension suggests this is a trend that cannot be ignored.

We know this ascension will happen, because cycling addresses so many challenges facing humanity. It reduces greenhouse gas emissions, traffic congestion, traffic accidents and the cost of medical treatment associated with today's sedentary lifestyles.[1] Compelled by these obvious benefits, cities across the industrialized world are developing plans that will make cycling a key plank of their transport strategies.

Then comes the peripheral dividends, which already are flowing to mature cycling cities like Amsterdam and Copenhagen, as well a relative newcomers like Portland, Oregon. The most lauded of these benefits are those that save or make money.[2] A 2011 report out of the London School of Economics estimates the economic benefit of cycling, to Britain's economy, has risen to 2.9 billion British pounds annually, thanks to early efforts by government to help cycling along.[3] The other surprise benefit, witnessed in Portland, is that cycling appears to have accounted for a slight overall increase in the number of journeys being made there, discretionary trips lubricating commerce and providing yet another unex-

1
*The Portland Bicycle Plan for 2030* provides a concise and easily downloadable summary of data supporting these claims, in section 1.1 'Making the Case for Investing in Bicycling'. Available HTTP: http://www. portlandonline.com/ transportation/index. cfm?c=44597&a=289122 (accessed 20 March 2011).

2
The cycling advocacy group Bikes Belong maintains an extensive and up-to-date index of studies that highlight the economic benefits of cycling. See http://www. bikesbelong.org/resources/stats-and-research/statistics/economic-statistics/ (accessed 20 March 2011).

3
Alexander Grous, 'Gross Cycling Product' Report, London School of Economics, August 2011.

4
A free to download lecture by Roger Geller, Bicycle Coordinator for the City of Portland, provides a pithy summary of the economic windfall Portland has enjoyed after spending as much on bicycling infrastructure as it otherwise might have on 1.5km of new freeway. Available HTTP: http://harangue.lecture. unimelb.edu.au/Lectopia/ casterframe.lasso?fid=2 04994&cnt=true&usr=n ot-indicated&name=not-indicated (accessed 25 October 2010).

5
Between 2006 and 2008, coinciding with Portland's growth in bicycle transit, the number of bicycle manufacturers making hand built bikes around that city rose from 5 to 17. Bicycle manufacturing and distribution contributed 17,126,578 dollars to Portland's economy during that period. Alta Planning + Design, *The Value of the Bicycle Related Industry in Portland*, September 2008. Available HTTP: http://www.altaplanning.com/App_Content/ files/fp_docs/2008%20 Portland%20Bicycle-Related%20Economy%20 Report.pdf (accessed 21 March 2011).

6
This claim, by Portland Mayor Sam Adams, and since repeated by Portland's Bike coordinator Roger Geller, has been scrutinized and found to be ostensibly accurate. See http://www.politifact.com/ oregon/statements/2011/ mar/19/sam-adams/ portland-mayor-sam-adams-says-portlands-spent-its-/ (accessed 16 February 2012).

7
Jonathan Bell, *Carchitecture: When the Car and the City Collide* (Basel: Birkhäuser, 2001).

pected monetary return on that city's investment in cycling.[4] Universal longings for health, mobility, a sustainable future, increased leisure time and simply more money forecast a rosy future for cycling.

The implications go beyond narrow lanes on the edges of roads and extend to how people recreate, dress and form social groupings. The example of Portland shows how a region can develop its own distinct cycling culture – in this case an incredible culture of handmade bicycle frame manufacturing[5] and a youth culture that revolves around cool bikes and brew pubs, rather than cars and drive-ins. Portland spent the same amount on its cycleway system that it otherwise would have spent on just 1.5 km of new freeway,[6] and now boasts a 5 to 10 per cent bike modal share (depending on who counts and how), which is many times the national average. Not content to stop there, they now have their sights set on those one-third modal share benchmarks set by Denmark and the Netherlands.

Idealists really are hoping for 30-fold increases in bike modal shares, from base rates of around 1 per cent in sprawling cities, to rates approaching those of dense and flat cities like Copenhagen and Amsterdam. They may never get there. Their bike modal shares may only double. That seems enough, though, for Portland, and fledgling cycling cities like London, San Francisco, New York and Melbourne, to become sites of bicycling spectacles: nude protest rides, valet bike parking, bike polo matches, cycle-specific clothing boutiques, enormous training or 'bunch' rides, bikes littering footpaths around bike-friendly cafés and tweed runs – a subtle new kind of protest event where large groups ride through the city in the dapper attire of the late 1800s, when cycling was a middle-class craze. Given some angle by which to claim minority status, it seems today's middle class will parade it; a mode of transport previously shunned now offers a perverse yet potent kind of prestige – not to mention genuine pleasure.

The ultimate – because it's expensive – expression of bicycle culture comes when this culture informs works of architecture. The result: 'bicycletecture' (for those willing to embrace neologisms). Bicycletecture is most readily understood if we think of it as the present day counterpart to 'carchitecture', a phenomenon of car-reliant urban expansion and the title of Jonathan Bell's 2001 book about buildings for cars.[7] Carchitecture propagandized for, made room for and drew inspiration from cars. Bicycletecture will propagandize for, make room for and draw inspiration from bicycles. We can be fairly sure architects will respond to the emerging bicycling boom in ways paralleling their forebears' responses to cars, because the templates for these three ways of thinking – propagandizing, accommodating, emulating – are still in place from the previous century, when they were settled upon as standard architectural responses to that era's car boom. By comparing and contrasting buildings for and about bikes, with buildings of the past century that were for and about cars, I'm hoping we will be braced for an imminent wave of architectural thinking.

Who are we who care about this? We are architects, developers, urban designers, planners, or anyone sufficiently au fait with the history of architecture to follow along. We don't need convincing that an age of bicycle transit is dawning, or that it will do more good than harm. We are more concerned with missing our chance to be agents of change at this critical time.

8
Filippo Tommaso
Marinetti, 'Futurist
Manifestor', in: R.W.
Flint (ed.), *Marinetti:
Selected Writings* (New
York: Farrar, Straus and
Giroux, 1972), 39-44. First
published in *Le Figaro*,
20 February 1909.

9
Antonio Sant'Elia,
'Messaggio', *Niove
Tendenze*, 1914.

### Cars and Bikes
### and Marinetti

Only two decades separated the bicycle craze of the 1890s and the phenomenon that was the Model T Ford, heralding a century of town planning and architecture predicated on private car ownership. However, before the First World War, both the car *and* the bicycle had been emblems of progress. Both were usurping horses, and motorists and cyclists alike were lobbying to have roads paved, or macadamized, to better suit tires. But only one vehicle would attain sufficient cultural standing to influence architecture. Vaticination of the car's ultimate triumph over the bicycle can be found in the Italian poet Marinetti's 'Futurist Manifesto' of 1909. Marinetti is driving his car when:

> Suddenly there were two cyclists disapproving of me and tottering in front of me like two persuasive but contradictory reasons. Their stupid swaying got in my way. What a bore! Pouah! I stopped short, and in disgust hurled myself – vlan! – head over heels in a ditch.[8]

Later in that manifesto, when we read of the world being enriched by the beauty of speed, and of a car being 'more beautiful than the Victory of Samothrace', we know Marinetti's tirade was sparked by two cyclists, with their sanctimonious looks, causing him to veer off of the road. The 'Futurist Manifesto', which has been said to have anticipated avant-garde sensibilities in the decades that followed, starts with a driver raging at two feeble cyclists, who had the gall to pass judgment on him. The rivalry has gone on, cars winning, thanks largely to the fossil fuel bounty.

While at first nebulous, it would not be long before the architectural and town planning implications of progressives' keenness for cars would come through in Antonio Sant'Elia's futurist manifesto for architecture, 'Messaggio'.[9] The street would not be a 'doormat' for buildings, but would 'plunge many stories down into the earth, embracing the metropolitan traffic . . . linked . . . by metal gangways and swift-moving pavements'. Sant'Elia's image is one of a mechanized built environment that, in hindsight, we know would largely be powered by the fuel that drove cars. In the 1920s, the USA alone would lay over 160,000 km of crude oil pipelines, for a nation buying Model T Fords at a rate of one every 15 minutes.

However, it was in Europe that the architectural implications of cars were being explored most creatively. Understanding the thinking behind avant-garde architecture for cars in interwar Europe helps us understand ways architects can begin to think about bicycles, in this age of the bicycle's comeback.

### The Delight of Buildings for
### Cars, Penguins and Bikes

Just as stables had to once be invented for horses, or as stations were invented for trains, new building types appeared in the 1920s for cars. We are thinking, to start with, of a purely utilitarian need. Of the many par-

top
Bicycle Rickshaw Service,
New York, NY
Photo: Mikael
Colville-Andersen

middle
Claes Oldenburg's *The
Sunken Bicycle* exposes
the significance of Le Parc
de la Villette to cycling in
this part of Paris.
Photo: Steven Fleming

bottom
Stuyvesant Town, New
York, NY
Photo: Steven Fleming

ticular examples of early buildings for cars, those that continue to interest architects all these years later tend to have married new programmatic demands to the progressive design ethos of the day, functionalism. The most salient aspect of Giaccomo Matte-Trucco's Fiat factory in Turin – engineer-designed and devoid of effeteness – is arguably its importance to architects. From the time it was championed in 1928 for its frankness by the early Italian Rationalists Gruppo 7 at their 'Esposizione dell'Architettura Razionale' in Rome, this car manufacturing facility has occupied a central place in the canon of modernist architecture. However, frankness alone does not quite explain why the Fiat factory has been so admired.

For his design of King Cross Station in London (1852), Lewis Cubitt has similarly been praised for allowing the shape of the railway sheds behind his façade to show through in an honest manner. Yet Cubitt's station occupies a relatively minor place in the architectural canon. Like Matte-Trucco's factory, it too borrowed cache from the most advanced transport mode of its day – that being the train. Yet it is hardly as famous. The difference is that utilitarianism, or frankness, in a building for cars showed itself capable, in Turin, of producing visually engaging sculptural forms, like a banked test track and helicoid car ramps. All utilitarianism in a railway terminus had been able to yield were two humdrum arches cut in a façade.

Additionally, the Fiat factory celebrates something about cars that cannot be said about trains: how cars are manoeuvrable. They may not be as nimble as ambulatory beings, but in the imagination of someone looking at Matte-Trucco's factory, cars can be personified. We can imagine cars circulating up and through the building as though with no drivers. Albert Laprade and L.E. Bazin's Le Marbeauf Showroom in Paris (1929) had the same kind of visual delight: the cars seemingly displaying themselves over six layers of car shelving facing a shop front.

One of the joys of looking at these otherwise utilitarian structures derives from the way we can imagine ourselves as being the car, asking: 'How would I drive to the roof?' The kind of empathizing being described is perhaps more obvious in something like Berthold Lubetkin's ramps for penguins at Regent's Park Zoo in London (1934). It is hard to look without putting oneself in the place of the penguins.

These examples demonstrate how circulation routes that have been optimally designed for modes other than walking invite us to imagine moving by uncommon means. With their Danish Pavilion at the 2010 Shanghai Expo, Copenhagen-based architects BIG engaged our imaginations in the same way; in this case by inviting us to imagine what it might be like to cycle our way through a building.

The cyclists' experience of the Danish Pavilion – which Ingels demonstrated in an online clip of himself riding through it[10] – was in profound sympathy with the dynamics of cycling. The ascent was gradual. Riders stopped and returned their bikes at the top, where their heart rates were highest and their speeds were lowest, making stopping more natural. As to the descent, it was wide, with lanes that merged gently, allowing a clear run to the ground. The energy conserving nature of bicycle movement was expressed as clearly in this temporary building in China as the raw power of the car is expressed in the Fiat factory's rooftop banked corners.

10
See http://www.
youtube.com/
watch?v=i99MzGa3Vec
(accessed 20 March 2011)

11
Adolf Loos, 'Ornament and Crime', in: Ludwig Munx and Gustav Kunstler (eds.), *Adolf Loos: Pioneer of Modern Architecture* (London: Thames and Hudson, 1966), 226-231. First published 1908.

12
Denise Scott Brown and Robert Venturi, 'On Ducks and Decoration,' *Architecture Canada* (October 1968), 48-49.

## Architecture that Propagandizes Driving or Cycling

Utilitarian design considerations around types of rolling provide a useful starting point for comparing bicycletecture with carchitecture. However, like works of art, works of architecture almost invariably embody ideas that transcend utility. BIG's Danish Pavilion contains many ideas, foremost a propaganda-filled message from Denmark to China. The building asserted the superiority of the bicycle over the car, thus inferring a wrong turn by China with its transit planning. This message was not simply stencilled onto the walls. That would be far too didactic. The architects also refrained from making digs at car culture, in the manner of James Wines's ironic proposals featuring parking lots with asphalt rolled over parked cars. The trick with modern architecture, ever since Adolf Loos made decoration so problematic,[11] has been to distort the whole building 'beyond the limits of economy and convenience'[12] – to quote one of Scott Brown and Venturi's critiques, of buildings reminding them of The Long Island Duckling.

What BIG did in Shanghai was to provide free bikes (which Expo visitors could borrow to explore the whole site) and place them on the roof of their building. If we wanted to be sober, we might say a more rational place for those bikes would have been the ground floor. But wouldn't that be a boring objection! Had the bikes been at the bottom, there would have been no reason to build spiralling ramps. And this in turn gave the building its visual delight and propagandist raison d'être. Although highly functional in the way they were rendered, those ramps did not serve a dry rational arrangement of spaces, but a layout driven by symbolic intensions.

Parallels can be drawn between the way BIG's pavilion advertised the bicycling lifestyle and the way Le Corbusier advertised life with a car in his design of the Villa Savoye (1929). Le Corbusier sized the overall structural grid of this house, and the radius of a ground floor curved wall, according to the turning circle of a Voisin car. That allowed drivers to enter the volume of the house in their cars, diagonally park in a garage, or drive right around and then exit. This does seem practical, until we realize a porte-cochere on the side of the Villa Savoye would have been a much cheaper solution, and might have saved a three point turn to enter the garage. Like putting bikes on a roof to justify ramps, bringing cars into the volume of the house proper to justify a road in the house is in some sense a ruse, its purpose to create architectural delight of the kind mentioned earlier in Turin and Regent's Park Zoo. All these examples not only accommodate, but glorify patterns of movement that are novel compared to human perambulation. In the tradition of the Villa Savoye, BIG's Danish Pavilion glorified the way bicycles move.

## The Significance of Moving Machines to Architecture

More probity can be gained at this juncture by considering whatever relationship exists between architecture and movement more generally. In the language of Jacques Derrida, movement can be thought of as an absent presence in architecture.[13] It is so conspicuous by its absence from architecture as to be the first thing one looks for when designing or beholding this most stationary art form. Among works of art, buildings are uniquely incapable of travelling to a new audience. It is we who must travel to them, as we do for example when we embark on an architectural pilgrimage.

The idea of transportation, we can thus say, is present in architecture the way speech is present in a piece of writing that serves as its stand-in. The wheels on the temple at Konark in India, the labyrinth on the floor of the cathedral in Chartres, fast looking buildings of the Streamline Moderne style: these and countless examples attest to a fascination among designers of buildings with the one thing their buildings cannot do themselves. They can't possibly move.

With that thought in mind, it is telling that the machines Le Corbusier held up as yardsticks of excellent design in *Toward an Architecture* – principally aeroplanes, ocean liners and cars – were machines of transportation. Famously, architectural commentator Sigfried Giedion would later speculate that modernist architects' interest in motion and machinery had been an appropriation of Einstein's special theory of relativity, according to which architecture has more than just three dimensions, the fourth being time.[14] According to Giedion, architects were following the lead of visual artists, like Picasso, whose late cubist works depicted subjects from two or more viewpoints on the one static canvas, thus capturing the time it would take one viewer to move between multiple viewpoints. Earlier still, futurist artists had been seeking to represent time, in their case by depicting subjects in motion, across time, in one stationary image. Duchamp's *Nude Descending a Staircase* is a well-known example.

In the context of the present discussion it is notable how often futurist artists made images of moving bicycles, not only cars. Alongside cars, bicycles might well have remained emblems of space-time had circumstances not so heavily favoured the car. But cars required no human effort to propel, they had available fuel in the ground waiting to be drilled and sold, and cars could cross a city more quickly than bicycles. Thus, as Jonathan Bell writes: 'In the minds of the world's most progressive architects, urban architecture was carchitecture.'[15]

It could hardly have been foreseen, in the interwar years, how those initial benefits would also lead to the slow demise of vehicular transportation; how saving humans from physical labour would adversely impact their health; how fuel supplies would soon wane and in their burning release greenhouse gasses; how cities would soon be congested with vehicular traffic; or how the bicycle might re-emerge as a cleaner, greener emblem of progress and potential yardstick for an art form that has long been looking to machines that move for its authority.

### Brownfield Reclamations:
### Key Sites for New Buildings for Bikes

All the possible cues bicycletecture might take from carchitecture will not be known until both modes of transport have been usurped by another, as yet not imagined. Until then, during the age of the bicycle, architects

13
Jacques Derrida, Of *Grammatology*, translated by Gayatri Chakravorty Spivak (Baltimore: Johns Hopkins University Press, 1976).

14
Sigfried Giedion, *Space, Time and Architecture: The Growth of a New Tradition* (Cambridge, MA: Harvard University Press, 1967).

15
Bell, *Architecture*, op. cit. (note 7).

13
Jacques Derrida, Of *Grammatology*, translated by Gayatri Chakravorty Spivak (Baltimore: Johns Hopkins University Press, 1976).

14
Sigfried Giedion, *Space, Time and Architecture: The Growth of a New Tradition* (Cambridge, MA: Harvard University Press, 1967).

15
Bell, *Carchitecture*, op. cit. (note 7).

might imagine whole cities along the lines of Le Corbusier's Plan Voisin of 1925, only this time for a society completely invested in cycling. Others might look to his Maison Citroën that, in theory at least, was to take its mode of production from the automobile industry. Could buildings be manufactured the way bikes are produced? These and other speculative projections will be returned to in later chapters, as will a question of equal gravity: If carchitecture provides templates for thinking about how bikes will inform architecture, are there precedents to help us anticipate *where* such works will occur?

Carchitecture is primarily a phenomenon of post-war urban sprawl. When we look at Google maps, we know the triple garages will be found in those residential areas with the long curving streets, designed to stretch out the traffic, and give drivers the illusion they have more road to speed down. Looking at figure/ground plans of urban districts, we know too that solid black dots on vast white fields represent cities where we would expect to find more car parking stations than we might find amid buildings that fill their whole sites. Most buildings for and about cars were built in areas that were planned for the car. So where should we look for architecture focused on cycling?

It would be naive to think bicycletecture will be defined in districts where cars look set to prevail. Some retrofitting for bike use might happen out there in car land; fuel prices might see some people swap their second cars for high-speed bicycles or velomobiles; but a counterpart phenomenon to carchitecture needs a counterpart urban fabric, conceived with bikes at the forefront of planners' thinking. The prospects at first would seem slight for that ever happening, given it is current best practice among urban planners to first optimize conditions for public transport and walking, and then allow for bikes secondarily.

However, it needs to be asked why places designed to be walkable aren't more like places that were built when everyone walked. Compare the figure ground plan of a medieval town with any urban design shrouded in its designer's own rhetoric about walkability and you will see the medieval town has the highest ratio of built form to open space, and that the urban fabric will be carved up by more streets, lanes and courtyards. There is an intimacy and pedestrian scale to towns from the days when people walked that seems impossible to recreate at this time, when we romanticize walking.

It seems society has not been prepared to sacrifice the space, light and fresh air that urban sprawl promised for the sake of truly walkable cities; we want, yet don't want, San Gimignano. Large-scale developers and financiers, who profit most when economies-of-scale can be leveraged, are another killer of walkable cities. The largest commercial, retail and residential projects are often the cheapest per square metre to build, have a gravity of their own that adds to the sales price and can be operated more efficiently too. Unto their own internal logic, these are smart buildings; they just don't come together to make walkable cities. So, for the foreseeable future, newly planned cities will not be as intimate and walkable as the medieval old towns we love to visit as tourists. We will be trying to build walkable towns; but the result will better suit cycling.

Early indications are that bicycletecture will principally be a phenomenon of large brownfield redevelopment sites, where planning for close
walkable towns, diluted by the suburban dream of more space, has created a kind of urbanism more suited to cycling. Some observant cyclists
would be aware of another boon to themselves from these kinds of sites,
stemming from the fact that brownfield sites usually belong to contiguous networks of current and former industrial land, with tendrils across
a whole city. A city's networks of mills, canals, docklands, rail corridors,
mines and the likes is its principal and most rational network. It is the
network that residential and commercial districts originally gathered
around.

The nearer cities come to redeveloping the whole of those former industrial networks with walkable public spaces, all linking up, the nearer
they will have come to creating a Utopia for cyclists, for whom all of
those new and proposed waterfront promenades, and legible pedestrian
boulevards, are not safe places to walk, but to ride. In the name of walkability (not ease of cycling), planners keep cars out of these areas, and
because the land follows such elements as waterways and the routes
of old rail lines, it tends to be flat. Flat and no cars: two things most
cyclists seek in their regular routes.

That those involved in the design process have focused on these
sites' walkability, and scarcely mentioned their cycling potential, should
not come as a surprise. Designers are, after all, only human, and only a
fraction of all humans regularly cycle in most modern cities.

### Revisiting Modernism

In an age of mass bicycle transit, even Le Corbusier's idea that a park
might be a city if all the activities could be discretely pushed into the
sky could be put back on the table. One of the infamous shortcomings
of the 'Towers in the Park' proposition was the defencelessness of the
ground plane. Unlike the low-rise perimeter blocks that cover most of
their site areas and have served cities well for millennia – by putting
eyes on the street for example – widely spaced towers put the community too close to the sky to keep a watchful eye over the ground. In
places where this model was used as the backbone of low-cost public
housing, those verdant parks Corbusier had been promising were soon
revealed as dangerous no-go zones. In more affluent areas, Corbusier's
parks became car parks.

In an age of mass bicycle transit, neither of those shortcomings
would be so pronounced. It goes without saying that parked cars, if
less people used them, would not be such a blight on the ground plane.
What does need spelling out, to the non-cyclist, is how unthreatening it
feels to be riding a bike, compared to walking. That feeling you can have
as a pedestrian, that eyes are following you, hardly exists when you're
cycling. You feel unapproachable. I appreciate that in poor, lawless cities criminals have been known to push cyclists onto the ground, with
the bald aim of stealing their bikes. However, this book is not addressed
to such contexts. In the First World, crime rates continue to fall, while

governments have learned the folly of concentrating public housing and thus making low-income ghettos. Automatically associating towers in the park with poor slums is completely unfair now.

I received my architectural education in the late 1980s, the high point of postmodernism, when most architects and planners were arguing for the return of the perimeter block. With Aldo Rossi's and Leon Krier's works as my inspiration, and Jane Jacobs' book as my bible, I went to work for Singapore's Housing and Development Board. By my supervisor's decree though, the ground planes of my schemes were conceived as pitiful parks. The buildings were all to be point-blocks – or, if aviation restrictions limited height, they would be slab-blocks. In either case, I was under strict orders to raise anything I designed one level off of the ground, as though the towers and slabs were magically hovering above a continuous park.

It was while I was engaged in this folly that I heard Jan Gehl speak at the National University of Singapore. The next week, our chief architect tore up a model I had presented him for his approval; he didn't like that my scheme incorporated a four-storey podium, framing an outdoor space like a room. That was the week I began planning an academic career.

I would never have believed then that I would one day see the good of modernist planning. But looking back on my time in Singapore, I can see how living in and adding to the world's stock of Corbusian slab blocks had softened my postmodernist stance. In a country where 87 per cent live in modernist style public housing and every last tower has an ethnic mix matching the national average – Lee Kuan Yew's trick to mix races – I saw for myself that high-rise public housing estates don't all have gangs patrolling the ground plane. The first place I lived was the prototype modernist town of Toa Payoh, a kind of Brasília. The problems that beset Pruitt-Igoe, I began to suspect, had less to do with the architecture than the non-representative concentration of disadvantaged inhabitants in that estate. The real lesson of Pruitt-Igoe, which had to be demolished just 14 years after it was hailed as state-of-the-art, was not that modernist buildings were wrong. It was that modernist architects could not be so sure of their predictions.

### Stuyvesant Town

But can't the same be said of urban designers who subscribe to today's orthodoxies? Can they really predict that better lives will result where there are perimeter blocks and streets framed by buildings as though streets are rooms? I know which I prefer – a room-like street or a park with towers – on Manhattan's Lower East Side. Riding my bike from Alphabet City (start-stop, start-stop), into Stuyvesant Town, is like escaping some kind of torture, one you had only told yourself you might love, because after all, this is New York, and I♥NY.

Stuyvesant Town is the outworking of a low site coverage ideology, first really pushed by Ebenezer Howard, that even today wins votes when expressed with the phrase 'open green space'. Jane Jacobs, and hundreds of urbanists that she has inspired, have paddled against the tide for 50 years now in an effort to make developers and buyers appreciate that another building close to your window doesn't automatically mean you live in a slum, that aimless green-space around buildings is worse than no green at all, and that certain private amenities are worth sacrificing for the sake of cosy, walkable neighbourhoods. I might have fought on Jacobs' side all my life were it not for my recent revelation, riding my bike around Stuyvesant Town.

Had I been walking, I know I would have held onto my postmodern prejudices. I would have thought Stuyvesant Town was boring, compared to the street life one block to the south on Avenue A. There are fewer shops activating the whole interior of Stuyvesant Town than the avenues have shops along any short block. But the shops lining the avenues go by as a blur when you're riding a bike. It is so pleasant, by contrast, to find the handful of shops spread around Stuyvesant Town appearing slowly enough for your eyes to register while moving at bike speed. Neither are there any blind corners out of which a child or other cyclists might quickly appear, on course for a collision. The winding paths give you a feeling of speed while hardly pedalling, yet plenty of space to anticipate the actions of everyone else (cyclists and walkers alike) on this non-vehicular ground plane.

The setting is not truly Corbusian, though. The buildings are only 11 storeys high, making their proportions more cubic than towering – I say this knowing height, in itself, can be inconsequential. It matters more that the buildings aren't raised on slender columns. While riding around there, I am reminded less of the Unité d'Habitation, with its dripping concrete-cancerous under croft, or Toa Payoh in Singapore where the 'void-decks' are even more miserable, than many university campuses I have ridden around. I'll mention a famous one: Harvard in Cambridge, Massachusetts.

While bicycling is not permitted in Harvard Yard, it is prolific on the main part of the campus, North of Cambridge Street, where the urban morphology – at least as it would appear in a figure-ground plan – is not dissimilar to that of Stuyvesant Town. There are buildings of roughly cubic proportions, with aimless green-space in between. Across that green are curved pathways, speaking of no higher aim than a cyclist or pedestrian heading to class. These are the key features of what I think of as a campus condition. This term exchanges pejorative associations with Pruit Igoe, which are conjured when we hear someone say 'towers in the park', for a seductive vision of bright young things, cycling and walking, with due regard.

### The Campus Condition

When large industrial tracts are redeveloped, a campus condition is the common result. Landmark edifices seem arranged like university faculty buildings and dorms on a broad cycling/pedestrian field, where anyone without a bike probably wishes they had one. Designers in the habit of driving or taking metros to places like these, then going around using their feet, would understandably have felt jealous of cyclists whizzing around them. If their jealousy turns into resentment, they are likely to have seen it as their role as designers to tame, stymie or even bar cyclists from entering.

But the large-scale financiers of these redevelopments do not seem inclined to build any smaller. They just don't care that pedestrians are dwarfed by the enormous size of a more profitable project or by the

16
Editors of Phaidon Press,
*Phaidon Design Classics*
(London: Phaidon Press,
2006).

relative vastness of the space between buildings, where streets are not designed in this instance to promote walking, but to provide broader outlooks to the apartments that frame them. If new streets were as intimate as the ones found in old, walkable cities, developers would have trouble selling their apartments. The fine-grained, human scaled, medieval town seems impossible to reproduce.

But what has been lost, if people are on the street, only instead of walking they are riding bikes? If only we were able to look at the bike-friendly city with the warmth we feel towards walkable ones, we might see that some things have been gained. Cyclists bring life to streets no less than pedestrians and can more easily be spread across a whole city, not only Main Street. The reach of their passive surveillance is all encompassing.

Places have more life, not less, when cyclists are encouraged to ride to them and through them; and they threaten nothing. University campuses, northern Italian towns like Ravenna, Dutch streets and other shared zones with high numbers of cyclists are living proof that cyclists and pedestrians quickly learn to share space with regard for each other.

Rather than harbouring jealously and having it manifest as antagonism towards people coming by bike, architects and planners doing work in these areas would be well advised to start cycling to site meetings, in that way developing the empathy they are going to need to help cycling flourish. If a designer feels he must drive, or take public transport, he might at least take a folding bike with him. The Brompton has a dignified air and design-world cache. Along with another compact bike, the Moulton F-Frame, the Brompton made it into *Phaidon Design Classics*.[16] The Strida didn't, but it is no less behoving of an architect's pride and station in life that in the present age would bide better as a vehicle to take to a site meeting than would a car.

### Bicycles are a
### Game Changer

From the time I started my career as an architect, and for the years I have researched and taught in the field, it has been the name of the game to build to street alignments, favour perimeter blocks, activate the street, put eyes on the street and make streets where pedestrians feel alive and secure. Break those rules with ground-floor apartments that need bars on the windows, cookie-cutter planning, minimal retail and everything else we find there at Stuyvesant Town, and you should get a ghetto, not people sunbathing in verdant bliss, as happens throughout the summer on Stuyvesant Oval.

The rise in numbers of cyclists provides scope to relax some of the strictures that flow from Jane Jacobs' thinking. There is hardly a moment when at least one bicycle isn't passing by Stuyvesant Oval. Likewise, you can't look anywhere around Harvard and not see somebody cycling. People who live or work in places like these are electing to ride rather than walk, both to save time and because riding is fun. Cyclists from elsewhere use these places as through-ways and in so doing activate public space the way vehicular through-traffic does not: with their living, uncovered faces and unshielded bodies.

Activating public space by encouraging cycling is not the uphill battle that activating space with pedestrians has proven to be. Pedestrians move slowly. They bunch up. Planners can't spread them around, so at best call on them to enliven main shopping streets and strips of cafés. But let's imagine a city where three quarters of trips are by bicycle, one quarter on foot, and cars are an oddity. Shops and cafés could be littered evenly across the whole city, just one at the base of each building. The Jane Jacobs ideal of throwing away zoning maps and encouraging a tossed-salad of functions might actually have some chance of succeeding.

# Cycle

# Because

# It's

# DESIGN

# Copenhagen

Bauhaus professors were scattered over America after the war, but the spirit and ideas of the Bauhaus drifted in a uniform column, due north from Dessau, to Copenhagen. A fine old home was waiting for them. The Royal Danish Academy of Fine Arts had been nurturing design culture since the 1700s, creating fertile conditions for a modernist scene.

One legacy of functionalist theory finding such a home as it did in Denmark is that average Danes revere their own best modern designers. 'Actually, we do want the Bauhaus in our house,' they would have said to Tom Wolfe, had Wolfe's rant against modernism, *From Bauhaus to Our House*,[1] been written to them instead of Americans. The Danes so love high modernist design that they preserve a hotel by Arne Jacobsen, their favourite son, such that not even the cutlery shall ever perish, but shall have eternal life: I am referring to the SAS Royal hotel, kept in every detail as Arne intended.

Another passion of the Danes – given their nation's flatness, and perhaps their Lutheran background – is cycling. When a love of bikes and of design comes together, iconic bike

1
Tom Wolfe, *From Bauhaus to Our House* (New York: Farrar, Straus & Giroux, 1981).

designs are an inevitable outcome. The BULLITT cargo bike, designed for speed and not comfort, is of Danish design. I personally own three retro-style roadsters by the Danish bike brand Velorbis, all contrived to look as though they have been based on sketches found in the diaries of Peter Behrens after his death. Meanwhile, the only bike brand ever to successfully carve out a designer-bike niche (with designer-bike price tags to match!) is the Danish brand Biomega, headed by acclaimed designer Jens Martin Skibsted. The world's first true velomobile, Carl Georg Rasmussen's LEITRA, is a Danish invention.

When bike lovers return from their pilgrimages to our holy lands (Denmark and the Netherlands) they frequently remark on how Dutch cycling has greater substance. Dutch vehicular traffic has been tamed more. Rarely, if ever, must cyclists stop and give way to cars in Dutch cities. Reports like these ignore how cycling in Copenhagen is so much more stylish than bicycling in the Netherlands! The Dutch may have the traffic

page 58
Copenhagen is recognised internationally by its blue bike lanes.
Photo: Michael Colville-Andersen

left
Bikes on the balconies of BIG and JSD Architects' VM Houses, Copenhagen
Photo: Michael Colville-Andersen

top right
Bullitt Cargo Bike
Photo: Mikael Colville-Andersen

bottom right
Transport cycling doesn't wait for the rain to stop.
Photo: Michael Colville-Andersen

design guidelines other nations may hope to have too by the end of this century, but the Danish ride with a fashionable air that we can all copy right now.

Copenhagen Cycle Chic is a runaway blogging phenomenon, franchised out to Cycle Chic bloggers in dozens of cities all over the globe. None can compete with the original though, for the simple fact that the original's author, Mikael Colville-Andersen, has such a wealth of material at his disposal every time he rolls onto the street with a camera slung over his shoulder. If you are tall, good looking and have ever ridden a classic style bike in Copenhagen (and let's face it, who in Copenhagen does not fit that description), you will probably have been photographed, without your knowing, for Colville-Andersen's blog. Rest assured, your privacy has been forsaken for a much higher cause. Upright cycling in office clothes is catching on faster worldwide than sports cycling did thanks to Lance Armstrong, or Mountain Biking did as a result of Gary Fisher's promotion, and this all thanks to you Copenhageners for appearing on copenhagencyclechic.com. Your style sense

in the saddle may be helping to reduce global warming – as your city's built fabric may be serving as a beacon to the rest of the world.

The consistency with which bike lanes have been introduced and blue paint has been striped across intersections makes Copenhagen one of the world's most recognizable, and copied, cities. That is why bike lanes on the curb side, not the road side, have come to be known as Copenhagen style lanes, even though similar bike lanes exist across half of Europe.

While blogs such as Cycle Chic have been exporting Copenhagen's city's image, architecture firms like Jan Gehl's have been exporting the sense that old buildings frame and look upon public space. But let's not forget that across almost half of Copenhagen that sense is reversed. Public space made from former docklands and dumps frames and looks

page 60 top left
Daily accurate counting of trips by bike in Copenhagen
Photo: Mikael Colville-Andersen

page 60 top right
Cyclists enjoying a beach day, Copenhagen
Photo: Michael Colville-Andersen

page 60 bottom right
Thoughtful conveniences incorporated into Copenhagen streets
Photo: Michael Colville-Andersen

right
The Åbuen Bridge, Dissing + Weitling Architects, 2008, completes a rail-to-trail bike route with sinuous curves that make this route unique among bike paths elsewhere in the city, Copenhagen.
Photo: Michael Colville-Andersen

pages 62 - 63
Sign indicating where cyclists should board in Copenhagen metro station
Photo: Michael Colville-Andersen

back towards buildings. People walk around, or more often ride around, a converted silo by MVRDV, a doughnut shaped dorm by Lundgaard & Tranberg, a glowing blue cube by Jean Nouvel . . . the list is endless. There is even a budget hotel out towards the airport designed by Daniel Libeskind – I stayed there a week and changed rooms three times before being allocated one that didn't make me feel as though I were trying to sleep in a museum.

Sure, I put style over substance in my choice of a hotel. But you Copenhageners would understand why. Style is a substance.

# Chapter 3

# Aesthetics, Modernism and Meaning

### The 'Machine Aesthetic'
### Looking to Bicycles

Today bicycles symbolize a range of ways in which late capitalism is being resisted. They are frugal with energy, both in their use and in their making. They allow individuals to take control of their health. They offer mobility, where increasingly cars offer hours trapped in traffic, plus fuel bills and frustration about finding some place to park. With their cultural ascension comes the natural inclination for designers to see bikes as yardsticks of excellence, the way Le Corbusier saw the car as a paragon of engineering perfection in *Towards a New Architecture*.[1]

An obvious place to look for works borne of the engineer aesthetic, where the inspiring machine is the bike not the car, are places where buildings have literally been built to serve cycling. Are there cases where architects of facilities for bicycles, have looked to the bicycles their buildings will house for design principles they too might apply?

Donal Paine of KPG Design Studio comes close. He is the architect of the Bikestation ('Bikestation' being the name of an American nation-wide franchise) outside Union Station in Washington. Paine describes this building's compressive arches, tied with closely spaced rods to the ground, as a reference to compressive bicycle rims, pulled on by stainless steel spokes. The reference is not merely cosmetic. The structure actually does behave like a bicycle wheel. However, on balance, this cannot be considered the building's central idea. Overwhelmingly, KPG's Bikestation is an expressive structure, recalling architectural design trends in the wake of Coop Himmelblau's rooftop office in Vienna. The architects have combined a sense of stylistic contemporaneity with curvilinear forms and transparency to provide the counterpoint necessary for this small building to exist comfortably beside its heavy rectilinear, Beaux-Arts style neighbour. Viewed in the light of that contextual challenge, Paine's bicycle wheel reference has the tone of a polite fiction. There is also no effort to imbibe the machine aesthetic, as nowhere would Paine claim the building stores bikes as efficiently as a bike performs its unique task. For KPG's Bikestation to be considered 'the bicycle of bicycle stations' – and by that I mean purely functional – it would more likely resemble the engineer designed bike storage system called eco-cycle by Japanese engineering firm Giken. Purely in terms of machine-like efficiency, an underground eco-cycle system trumps KPG's Bikestation many times over, using robotics to automatically deposit bikes in mere seconds.[2]

A type of structure that is even more wheel-like than the one used for KPG's Bikestation has been employed to build roofs over numerous velodromes such as Dominique Perrault's in Berlin. It features a compressive continuous edge band (analogous to a bicycle rim) resisting the pull of radial members or trusses (spokes), that can be engineered to be shallower because they are in constant tension. However, with roofs of this kind having progenitors as old as the valorium roof of the Coliseum in Rome, any associations architects might draw between such a roof on a velodrome and the design of a bicycle wheel should again be viewed

1
Le Corbusier, *Towards a New Architecture* (London: Architectural Press Limited, 1927).

2
It warrants mentioning that cyclists in Tokyo were unable to retrieve their bikes for days following the major earthquake there in 2011. Trains were likewise not working. Indications from web sources are that many bicycle stores had sold all of their floor stock by the end of the day, to people facing three-hour walks to their homes.

images clockwise
Michael Ubbesen
Jakobsen's BauBike
Courtesy of Michael
Ubbesen Jakobsen

Renovo Pandurban
Laminated Bamboo
Commuter
Courtesy of Ken Wheeler,
Renovo Bikes

Renovo bike factory,
Portland, OR
Photo: Steven Fleming

Biomega brand bike, by
Danish industrial designer
Jens Martin Skibsted
Photo: Mikael
Colville-Andersen

Biomega brand bike, by
Danish industrial designer
Jens Martin Skibsted
Photo: Mikael
Colville-Andersen

Renovo R4 black Walnut
and Port Orford cedar bike
Courtesy of Ken Wheeler,
Renovo Bikes

with some scepticism, more as rhetoric than a true account of where they found their ideas.

Seen beside hollow and stretched analogies to the bicycle wheel, it seems a pity some of the deepest affinities between architecture and bicycle design are ones architects have, until recently, been neglecting to sell. Consider Ryder sjph Architects, who boast how the dome of their Sydney Olympic Velodrome weighs 40 kg per $m^2$, a record low relative to its 100-m span. Yet they make nothing of the fact that performance bikes too are designed to be as lightweight as possible. Neither do they relate the computer modelling of their building's natural convection systems to similar modelling done of cyclists and their bikes to reduce wind drag. In both cases, state of the art science at the design stage makes objects (buildings and bikes) as frugal as possible with their energy inputs.

However, one decade later, opportunities like these are not being missed. Of their Olympic VeloPark in London, Hopkins Architects says on its website:

> Cycling inspired the concept for the Velodrome. The bike is an ingenious ergonomic object, honed to unrivalled efficiency; we wanted the same application of design creativity and engineering rigour . . . to manifest itself in the building. Not as a mimicry of the bicycle but as a three dimensional response . . . focused on the performance and efficiency of every aspect of the building.[3]

One hundred and twenty years of relentless refinement has seen the bicycle evolve into an energy efficient machine par excellence, epitomizing many of the design principles to which architects now aspire with their work. According to the website of Seattle-based architect firm Velocipede: 'Bicycles embody the principles of sustainability, that buildings would do well to emulate.'[4] We can imagine Velocipede's clients reiterating this message to guests coming to their new architect-designed house, saying it is like a bicycle in its frugality; such are the mechanisms via which positive associations flow in a field where rhetoric can transform a roof over ones head into a concretization of their most lofty ideals.

### Bikes in the Sky

In recent bicycling architecture we can see a renewed interest among architects in another of their discipline's preoccupations from the modernist era, and that is the desire to literally lift public life off of the ground. The rebirth of this old modernist dream, being spurred on by bikes, begins with BIG's Danish Pavilion in Shanghai – discussed in the previous chapter. Another Danish firm, JDS Architects, that has strong ties with BIG, is now hoping to build a larger and permanent version of the Danish Pavilion in a new district of Shanghai being hailed as 'Bike City'. As part of their Bike City master plan, JDS is proposing a number of buildings. As well as the spiralling ride-through museum inspired by the 2010 Danish Pavilion, there is a hall with a stepped green roof reminiscent of a jelly popped out of an old Indian stepped pond, if such

3
See http://www.hopkins.co.uk/projects/_3,131/ (accessed 23 March 2011).

4
See http://www.velocipede.net/aboutus/ourName.html (accessed 13 December 2010).

a thing could be used for a mould. Where stepped ponds invite all walks of life down into the earth, to the water, here a positive cast thrown from that mould would invite bike riders to meet in the sky.

The boldest vision for a cycling track into the sky has been Carlo Ratti's (unrealized) London Cloud, a proposal he put forward for the 2012 London Olympics. Like the ride-through bicycling museum proposed by JDS in Shanghai, this too would have comprised floor plates in the form of a double helix, separating cyclists ascending from those speeding downward. While architecture knows earlier helicoids – the Minaret of Jam in Afghanistan for example, or the car park underneath Sydney's Opera House – the form seems poised to meet with its ideal function, should circulation for bikes become a big deal in the future.

Could bike circulation take off as a generator of new building types? Would there be anything to be gained? Looking at another building by BIG, 8-House in Ørestad, an urban renewal district on the Southern edge of Copenhagen, we can say bike circulation has enormous potential.

8-House is a giant perimeter block, pinched at the waist to make a figure-eight form. Where in regular slab blocks apartments are arranged floor upon floor, each floor with its own access corridor linked to others via a lift, BIG uses the extraordinary length of this perimeter block to array apartments along a continuous and gradual rise. The access balconies serving those apartments are like switchback mountain roads, running uninterrupted from the ground to the roof.

Such access routes might be dubious propositions were it not for Copenhageners' fondness for cycling. Few residents would walk hundreds of metres sideways just to go up one level. They would use the stairs or the lift. With a bicycle though, moving sideways is easy, lifts present difficulties and stairs are intolerable. A resident wheeling a bicycle out of his or her apartment would naturally turn and ride down the ramp, rather than use the lift. Even on the home leg, few regular cyclists would be so daunted by the slight uphill gradient that they would take the lift instead of riding the ramp back to their door. Once a whole population has added bicycles to their bodies, like prostheses, ramps become a viable means of vertical circulation in buildings.

The triumph of 8-house is that the bike ramp actually functions, programmatically, socially and mechanically replacing motor driven cables with human powered bike chains, as the things lifting people though buildings. The old story that tall buildings could never have happened had it not been for Elisha Otis's plummet-proof elevator of 1852 really ought to be reconsidered. Tall buildings could exist with, instead of lifts, people winching themselves to the top on bikes, up these kinds of ramps.

Another narrative that stands to be changed due to 8-House is that of the street in the sky. Announced by Le Corbusier, it never quite gelled because 'streets' like the one in the Unite d'Habitation in Marseilles (1946–1952), with offices, shops and a hotel, were disconnected from streets on the ground. As streets go, Le Corbusier's streets in the sky worked about as well as the streets of Manhattan would work if the avenues were all taken away and the only way of moving from one street to the next was via the subway. The mere suggestion is maddening, yet precisely what Le Corbusier was promoting when he said an access corridor reached via the dark vortex of a passenger lift would somehow be an aerial street. The experiment – repeated with every new lift-access condo – seems poised every time to collapse into chaos of the kind J.G. Ballard imagined in his dystopian novel *High-Rise*.[5]

8-House gives new life to the old dream of aerial streets by creating an access balcony more like a mountain pass than separate streets scattered across an archipelago of little islands. Admittedly, cyclists don't have an express route or 'avenue' via which to move vertically in the quick manner one moves north and south in Manhattan. Residents of 8-House have to crisscross their way to the top; but as they do, their experience is of an access balcony far more like a street, with the opportunities a continuous street affords to interact with anyone in a building, not just those who happen to live on your floor.

The New Brutalists in England – Peter and Alison Smithson, and a generation of government architects – were enamoured by Le Corbusier's late works, and looked for alternative ways to use reinforced concrete technology to raise the street up off of the ground. In the Smithson's case the idea was packaged as part of a vast Utopian vision, a city-wide pedestrian plane one level up from the traffic below. If every new urban building in London could be given an entry at the level of the Smithson's proposed noble plane, neighbouring terraces could all be made to join up. Pedestrians could go about their lives without ever crossing a road.

A number of projects designed according to this principle are scattered around London – The Barbican, London Wall, the National Theatre – each still waiting for neighbouring properties, and their neighbours in turn, to be redeveloped with a Smithson style terrace. They look as though they will be waiting forever, the legacy of a consensus that was doomed to never be reached. Anyone whose curiosity has ever lured them, against gravity, up the stairs and onto one of these terraces knows how ghostly and foreboding they nowadays feel.

What if those terraces were not reached via stairs by pedestrians, but via ramps and on bicycles? In effect, BIG's ramp at 8-House is a Smithson style/New Brutalist terrace, only it is not detached from the ground. Any sense that entry is at ones peril, at least if they do not wish to be mugged, is dispelled by the knowledge that this particular street in the sky belongs to a network of streets including the rest in the building and all those of Copenhagen down on the ground. Passers-by could appear from any direction – and quickly, if they were riding a bike.

Speaking of cyclists being good for pedestrians highlights a fundamental difference in attitudes towards bikes in Denmark as compared, for example, to England. In preparation for the New Brutalists' grand elevated terrace, a bylaw was enacted in England in 1967 that prohibited any kind of 'vehicle', and that included bicycles, from coming onto those public walkways.[6] As written, bikes could not even be walked there – but then neither could one play a musical instrument or sit on a balustrade. New York's Highline, the elevated greenway to which the world is now looking, has similar rules, stifling activity to assuage the overblown fears of a few vocal killjoys.

5
J.G. Ballard, *High-Rise* (London: Jonathan Cape, 1975).

6
BYELAWS made under Section 12 of the City of London (Various Powers) Act 1967, by the Mayor and Commonalty and Citizens of the City of London, acting by the Common Council, with respect to City Walkways.

While it is not unknown for pedestrians to complain about cyclists in Copenhagen, there at least bicycles are not legally viewed as things more like motorized vehicles than people on foot. Bike lanes grow out of the footpath, not out of the road. Bikes pass on the footpath side of parked cars, leading Jan Gehl to frequently quip that his city uses parked cars to protect cyclists, not visa versa. Add to this people's familiarity with bikes and their relaxed way of shifting over if they hear a bike bell, and we can understand the access balconies of 8-House being enlivened, not spoilt for pedestrians, as a result of bicycle access.

On the one hand, 8-House reflects conventional wisdom about perimeter blocks, green roofs and putting commercial space on the ground floor. Its circulation, however, reminds us of images of the Tower of Babel, or explanations of how the Egyptians got stones to the top of the pyramids. All prior attempts to make apartment buildings more social now look exactly like that: like attempts. Factor in the explosion of bicycle transport all over the world, and as a cycling enthusiast I believe we are looking at a major addition to the architectural canon.

It would be good for sale prices if that proved to be true. Just as most residents of Marseilles don't vie to live inland and 8-km south of the port (where the Unite d'Habitation is sited), Copenhageners are similarly disenchanted by the location of 8-House – that is its similar distance south of their city centre, and its location at the far end of an urban renewal project that was less than one-quarter of the way built when the global financial crisis placed further works on indefinite hold. As a real estate proposition, the Unite d'Habitation just ticks along, because great design means enough to some buyers that they are prepared to overlook things like mean housing prices. To live there is to maintain a private conversation with Le Corbusier every time you open a window, and to be available to converse in like manner with likeminded residents and architectural pilgrims. Personally, I would not move to Copenhagen unless I could be assured an apartment in 8-House, opening onto that access balcony, for all the same reasons people live in Le Corbusier's building – oh, and so I could put all my bikes on display.

### Between Art for Art's Sake and Art for Utility

Though the machine aesthetic is an influential idea within architecture, seldom has it legitimized buildings with no sense of style, although this was not Le Corbusier's plan. If we look at the machines to which he points, they are not machines hidden from sight. All of them, especially cars, had styling, or features, purely for looks' sake. On this front, Le Corbusier was no different than most of his architect peers, who were happy for style trends in car design to cross over to architecture. During the art deco period, when this was most rampant, buildings were treated with grills, finials and sports striping; the Chrysler building has its own panelling. Then, in the post-war period when cars were being designed to look like the flying craft it was imagined everyone would soon use to commute, architects responded with fittingly fanciful Googie style buildings.

Architecture's less rational aspects suggest its exponents would never swap a fantastic emblem for one that just does the job. Maybe bicycles are not evocative enough to ever take the place of cars in architects' imaginations?

According to one of cycling's most prominent ambassadors, Mikael Colville-Andersen of Copenhagen Cycle Chic fame, everyone in Copenhagen cycles, but none would identify himself as a 'cyclist' per se, that being a moniker that is only used in non-cycling cities. He claims Copenhageners therefore take a quotidian view of their bikes. Their bikes, he argues, are as invisible to them as their vacuum cleaners or washing machines.

Of course there is some truth to this observation. Little effort is made to guard most bikes from theft. Danes whose bikes are stolen can claim the cost of a replacement with just a few clicks on the police department's and their insurer's web pages. Yet evidence of bike love, over and above any known form of appliance fixation, can be found on Colville-Andersen's own Cycle-Chic blog: photos of bicycles adorned in ways no one would ever adorn washing machines. One of Colville-Andersen's own bicycles is a red Bullitt cargo bike, hardly the choice of someone not projecting an image. His own and his followers' growing chorus of Cycle-Chic blogs make it abundantly clear that even citizen-cyclists use their bikes to project an image, in the same way people project an image using their clothes, or, for that matter, their cars. Not even Communist China could say bikes were not designed as objects of evocation and pride, when new Flying Pigeons glitter with head badges and chrome.

Concomitant trends in architecture and bicycle design have long reflected sensibilities current across those and other fields of design. Consider the following 'coincidences': how Buckminster Fuller was developing space-frame buildings in the same era as Alex Moulton was developing space-frame bicycles; how Calatrava's formative works circa 1990 coincide roughly with the Slingshot bicycle's best years of sales, each having cables instead of ridged members in tension; how Zaha Hadid and bicycle designers working with monocoque carbon are currently exhibiting a similar taste for sinuous forms and enamel-like finishes; and how bike builder Craig Calfee's spider web frame was a highlight of the North American Handmade Bicycle Show not long after LAB had built Federation Square in Melbourne, Australia – both look the same.

No matter if causative connections could ever be drawn, these examples at least dispel doubts that bicycle design sits outside of design culture. Its exponents are as informed as car designers and architects of the visual languages that are shared across all design fields.

### Buildings, Bicycles
### and the Art World

Bicycles can even be art. Of all artefacts with a use, bikes and buildings are among a few types that are capable of being so laden with meaning as to no longer be concerned with their use, having gone past a tipping point where art takes over from utility. The focus here is not on found objects like Duchamp's *Fountain* (1917) or that same artist's *Bicycle*

*Wheel* (1913), an assemblage that included part of a bike. Rather, we are looking at whole bikes, on their own, that are primarily about something other than transportation, and buildings in which art-world thinking is so strong that they are less about shelter than some deeper message.

A few of the low-rider bicycles David Byrne chose to include in an exhibition he curated in 2009 at Aldrich Contemporary Art Museum in Ridgefield, Connecticut were so low the pedals would hit the ground should one try to ride them. We wonder what these bikes could be about if not transportation, and shift our attention to Hispanic-American youths, pimping their bike rides because they don't have the money to get noticed with cars. The art world looks for that deeper meaning, just as it looked for something other than pot scourers in Andy Warhol's fake boxes of Brillo Pads. By contrast, the cycling world looks for performance, so only sees a useless contraption.

At its own extreme limits of artiness, architecture sacrifices utility to the same end: as a way of foregrounding meaning. Peter Eisenman designs spaces that cannot even be accessed, as he did with House 11a, as a tactic to get viewers to think with him about the nihilistic course of humanity. A door in House VI swings shut but does not close its doorway, in this case to encourage viewers to think about the workings of signification, how they are looking at a sign of a door, rather than something with a door's function. Architecture and bicycle design occupy a similar space, poised between fine art at one extreme end and pure utilitarianism at the other. It is in the middle ground between those polarities, that we can see a particular affinity between architects and designers of a new wave of chic bikes for urban commuters.

### Designerly Bikes

Renewed interest in bicycle transit, especially in creative centres, is inspiring designers (many of whom would have sat beside student architects when taking classes on twentieth-century design history, or materials properties) to design production bikes of their own. Examples are Michael Ubbesen Jakobsen's *BauBike* and Christophe Robillard's *Victor Bicycle*. Both bikes pay a stiffness and weight penalty for the sake of designer qualities, of the kind any architect would instantly recognize. Celebrated architects are just as ready as bike designers like these to compromise when it comes to practicality, if it means realizing works with more visual interest and clarity.

Designer Jens Martin Skibsted came to the realization that bicycles could compete directly with luxury cars if instead of attempting to make them faster or lighter, design world thinking came into play and the problems of everyday urban mobility were solved in witty and elegant ways. When Skibsted tells the story of the birth of his bike brand Biomega, he begins with accounts of a holiday in Barcelona, looking at architecture. Skibsted was studying philosophy, admiring buildings and compulsively sketching various bicycles, some of which are now design icons if not design classics.

Architect Bjarke Ingels, who rides a Biomega to his office in Copenhagen and who didn't even own a car before he opened his second office in New York City, has entered into a partnership with Skibsted called

<u>top</u>
BIG, 8-House, Copenhagen
Photo: Steven Fleming

<u>left</u>
Highline from an elevated
position, New York, NY
Photo: Iwan Baan

<u>middle</u>
Craig Calfee's spider web
frame
Courtesy of Calfee Design

<u>right</u>
Federation Square,
Melbourne
Courtesy of Alex Ivanov

<u>bottom</u>
JDS Architects, the hall
of 'bike city', Shanghai
(unbuilt)
Courtesy of JDS Architects

KiBiSi. It is a conspicuous affiliation, symptomatic of a groundswell of interest in bicycles among architects and designers, not as pieces of sporting equipment but as emblems of a worldview that informs how they look at design and the city.

One of the heaviest, slowest, but aesthetically most delightful bicycles that will ever be produced on a large scale was designed by Dutch landscape architects West-8. When their proposal for Governor's Island in New York Harbour is fully realized, visitors will spend time there availing themselves of regular park amenities (toilet blocks, pathways, park benches), plus 3,000 wooden bikes scattered around for free use, each resembling a bird. There could be something almost alchemical about a park where rolling/flying is as free and natural as breathing, or summoning a trained bird to come give you a ride. Wood may be an impractical material from which to build bikes, but it also connects riders with the wooded environment that will exist on the island. The philosophy of phenomenology is evident here on more levels than could normally be hoped for in architecture, due to one inspired gesture. Bikes have been incorporated in an architectural response in a way that makes them as integral as any fixed object.

Someone who would disagree that wood is necessarily an impractical material for a bicycle frame is Ken Wheeler, the founder of Renovo Bicycles in Portland, Oregon. Wheeler builds high-performance bicycles from glue-laminated timber. The material is computer routed, inside and out, into shapes almost indiscernible from high performance carbon framed road bikes and mountain bikes. The completed bikes are roughly 1 kg heavier than carbon frame bikes, but otherwise are benchmarked against them. They are just as stiff laterally, equally strong and in most ways more durable. The result is a high-performance bicycle with the natural beauty of wood and an eerie ride quality. There is virtually no road noise, the wood naturally dampening vibrations and moreover providing an existential connection to an organic material, with the story of its making visible through a glass smooth epoxy finish. A disproportionately high number of buyers, Wheeler reports, are architects.

Renovo is one of a handful of Portland based brands represented by a unique trade show room, the Het Fairwheel Podium in Portland, which is ran like a private art gallery. When the Spin Light Bike, a one-off creation that set a world minimum weight record for a fully functioning geared bicycle (2.84 kg), became famous internationally, Het Fairwheel Podium was its 'art' dealer, even dismissing a particular bidder, who arrived by private jet with an open cheque book to buy it, because he knew too little about bicycles to be considered a suitable owner/collector. High-performance bicycle frames, hand painted by well-known artists, are dealt with in similar fashion.

When architects design bikes, we can often see in the results evidence of their discipline's longstanding enthusiasm for truth and integrity in the way materials are expressed in their 'as-found' state, an idea echoed in the words of seminal figures ever since Ruskin. The Mora folding bike is a good example of the normative values shared by most architects, being exhibited in the design of a bike. It is made using stainless steel box sections and finely cut stainless steel plate, brushed not painted. Josep Mora, the bike's Spanish industrial designer, trained as an architect. Looking at his unpainted bike, we're reminded of how Louis I. Kahn would say buildings should tell the story of their own making.

The Mora folding bike is an exquisite example of an architect advertising principles that hold for all of his work, in the mobile, mass marketable form of a bike. It is an example of an architect doing with bikes what heroes of the mid twentieth century often did using chairs. A bike built by architect and industrial designer Ron Arad as a one-off to raise money for the Elton John AIDS Foundation has rose-like wheels made from bent steel. The wheels recall the centrepiece sculpture Arad designed for his Atelier Notify in Milan and the roof he designed for the 'Mediacite' shopping centre in Liege, Belgium. They are hardly the most functional bicycle wheels, providing no traction and a deafening clatter, but as is the case with many 'designer' products – take Rietveld's chair for example – that utility is consciously compromised to foreground something that will intrigue those who follow design trends.

Another architect to express aspects of his design thinking using a bike is Andrew Maynard in Melbourne, Australia. His OLC bike is conceived as a frame and wheels punched from a single sheet of ply, to be flat-packed and sold for not much more than a cheap helmet. Again, a virtue is made of raw plywood and how it would be CNC routed to make what Maynard claims would be the world's cheapest bike. So far, unfortunately, it has done more laps of the blogosphere than the street, and has yet to be prototyped, despite all the digital press. It is hardly surprising though that a proposal like Maynard's should enjoy 15 minutes of global fame via Twitter and blogs. It strikes a note with people concerned about poverty. It spreads values shared among design world initiates, and if in fact it is ever made, it could be produced using renewable resources and less embodied energy than would normally go into a bike.

At this time when hardly an architect alive would forego any opportunity to cloak their practice with environmental awareness, for example by borrowing a piece of the bicycle's green credibility, some, as one might imagine, have been fabricating bike related projects in their spare time. Czech architect firm H3T has built a bicycle drawn sauna. It is available for cyclists to hire in Prague, attach to their bikes and take some place nice, like the river. In the tradition of the modernist chair, this tiny object attempts to capture principles the firm applies on a larger scale to its buildings.

The Tokyo-based husband and wife team of architects, Atelier Bow-Wow, have built four bikes, resembling rickshaws, that can be backed together in such a way that rearward facing seats towed behind each form a temporary living room, on the street. Entitled 'Furnicycle', the installation was originally made for the 2002 Shanghai Biennale. The architects were inspired by temporary gatherings on neighbourhood streets in Beijing, where people arrange furniture throughout the day. Chinese authorities have been moving to stamp out the custom; Furnicycle is Atelier Bow Wow's way of subtly protesting. In the context of the preceding passages, Furnicycle is most notable though for bringing together three phenomena in one work: the bicycle as art, in a gallery; the works of architects conceived as pieces of art; and the bicycle assuming a role formerly performed by architects' chairs.

# Cycle
# Because
# It's
# PRESTIGIOUS
# Sydney

In Sydney, nobody asks, they just take. It has been this way since Captain Cook sailed into the harbour. He didn't come with beads or trinkets to trade. He saw the existence of prior inhabitants as a trifling concern that he could simply ignore.

The settlers who followed Cook didn't chart the course of their own roads. They just widened the trails that were already there, following ridgelines and tread by aboriginals for thousands of years. Now these are Sydney's arterial roads. When it came to finding lime to make mortar, the builders of the present city mined the aboriginals' mountains of oyster shells, called their 'middens'. No one quite knows how the Cadigal tribe felt about being treated as though they didn't exist.

In the light of this history of taking, it's hard to get too upset about cars hogging roads that were originally built for pedestrians. Cyclists, it seems to me, have the least right of anyone to be complaining, since in the latest occupation they are the culprits. Deciding the law is absurd for expecting them to ride on hostile roads, they have started to 'slow-cycle' on footpaths. They didn't wait for permission. They just moved in and took over.

Cyclists are even taking notes from Captain Cook's military cunning. Rather than battling for space against people armed with modern weapons (cars, in this case), cyclists are taking on the defenceless. They don't have to hurt, or even bully, those using the footpath for walking; they just nuzzle them over. The laws here are irrelevant and moreover unenforceable. Sydney exists for the taking, by whoever is most desperate to have it, and right now commuters are urgent. Trains are overloaded, cars are all stuck in jams. Despite all its contortions in deference to car flow, the footpath is the quickest option and is just that much quicker again for those who elect to take bikes.

The groundswell of bike use is reflected in local government, where independent Mayor Clover Moore has started creating a network of bike paths on the pedestrians' side of parked cars. Intrepid cyclists are welcome still to assert themselves in the traffic. Their rights haven't been challenged. What the local government is saying is that anyone who might have otherwise walked on the safe side of parked cars now has the option of pedalling there as a way to get to work faster.

This new approach has brought Sydney's inner-city residents and their local representatives into conflict with government departments, whose jurisdictions cover more than 130 other local government electoral zones across New South Wales. The Roads and Traffic Authority (RTA) – who, as their name suggests, are mostly focused on car flows – have said that if cyclists want to move with pedestrians, they can jolly well wait with pedestrians at every crossing. Their own design guidelines and rulebooks treat cyclists as suicidal operators of the flimsiest 'vehicles' allowed on the road, for whom the door-zone is safe enough, and road shoulders of no guaranteed width can be counted as bike 'lanes'.

Yet despite this latent hostility towards cyclists in the way roads are designed, most Australians believe their government leads the world in the protection of cyclists, because they have introduced mandatory helmet laws. Clover Moore has asked that these laws be reviewed. She's one of a minority of Australians who understands why such laws have been rejected elsewhere for doing more overall harm than they do good. Meanwhile citizens wanting the right to ride without helmets respond as they respond to everything else: simply

page 78 top
Bikes appear incidentally in pre-Second World War street scenes, such as this one in blue-collar Newcastle.
Courtesy of the State Library of New South Wales

page 78 bottom
'Clover Moore' style cycle lanes, Sydney
Photo: Gus Potts

left
Lower part of Johnston's Creek, Sydney
Photo: Gus Potts

right
Johnston's Creek continues with space for future path development
Photo: Gus Potts

left
Council makes footpath
cycleway, angry graffiti,
cyclist rides anyway,
Surry Hills, Sydney
Photo: Gus Potts

right
Bike shop on
cycleway, Sydney
Photo: Gus Potts

page 81
Restrictions/separation
of cyclists/pedestrians
on Harbour Bridge
cycleway, Sydney
Photo: Gus Potts

pages 82 - 83
Entry to Harbour Bridge
cycleway, Sydney
Photo: Gus Potts

by taking. Conscientious objectors claiming the right to ride without helmets exist in numbers police can't contend with.

The overthrow of helmet laws and the takeover of footpaths foreshadow potentially much bigger contests, as cycling increases in political power. Managers of rail infrastructure will come under pressure to do more than simply provide bicycle parking at stations. Easements, along which passenger trains currently run, will need to double as easements for express bicycle routes.

There are disused rail tunnels underneath Sydney, the longest intersecting St James Station, right in the middle of town. An architecture firm in New York called RAAD is developing a fibre optics based system that could be used to fill this tunnel with real sunlight and trees.[1] Cyclists could fill it with eyes.

Cycle space is so often space that has been neglected that discovering opportunities to expand it can be as simple as exploring the upper reaches of creeks and drains. The

lower portions of Johnston's Creek, near the harbour, have bike paths and restored natural habitats. Further upstream the creek disappears into concrete lined culverts that people blindly pollute, forgetting they're polluting the harbour. As cycling grows, it could provide the impetus for acquiring property spanning those drains, to extend bike paths further upstream, remediating creeks in the process. A waterway people enjoy because there is a bike path is one they will care for and one that will transport more people than litter.

1
See http://delanceyunderground.org/ (accessed 16 November 2011).

2
See http://www.greenway.org.au/ (accessed 6 February 2012).

Greater Sydney will soon have a greenway from Cooks River in the South West, to Iron Cove on the harbour. The obvious bike route from Iron Cove to the city would follow the edge of the water, much of it floating, just beyond the private jetties of people living on the harbour in Balmain and Birchgrove. When enough people are cycling to elect their own governments, they will see the existence of private jetties as a trifling concern that they can simply ignore, as Captain Cook would have.

# Chapter 4

# Staking Out Cycle Space for a Bicycling Empire

**Cars Won by Their Status,
Not by Their Might**

The displacement of bicycles by cars in our cities may seem like a post-war event, but photographic evidence suggests it was already happening in the 1930s and 1940s. Or, more accurately, old photos tell us it was during the interwar period that bicycles were being outclassed by cars. Photographs from the time of central business districts throughout the First World show there were surprisingly few bicycles in our cities back then; and this well before the era of drive-in movies and houses with fewer windows facing the street than garage doors. What we find in old photos of city centres are cars, certainly many pedestrians, plus busses and trams.

Old photographs in which there are bicycles are of industrial towns and blue-collar neighbourhoods. Out in those areas bikes were an inconspicuous yet ubiquitous presence; that ubiquity, if anything, was underlined further by the way bikes were so rarely the focus of a photographer's gaze. They just happen to be in each shot.

We are told from old photos that wherever people gathered in the 1930s and 1940s, someone would be there on a bike; unless the gathering took place in 'the big smoke': in central business districts greater class-consciousness seems to have dictated to white-collar workers that riding a bike was demeaning. Business attire was a matter of decorum here, determining travel in the sheltered confines of a bus, tram or train, or ideally by car if ones station and income allowed.

Standard histories concerning the take-over by cars focus on physical factors like lane widths, volumes of cars on the road, urban sprawl making cities too vast to cycle, death rates and other factors like these that would naturally lead parents not to allow their kids to cycle to school. But in my own blue-collar city, whole road lanes were filled with thousands of men riding bikes to and from our local steelworks with each change of shift. No one believes for a moment that car drivers could have bullied tough bike riders like these off of the road altogether. An account of the bicycle's eclipse by the car is needed that goes beyond physical impediments and addresses questions of decorum, perception and most pointedly class.

Told in class terms, the story of bicycle commuting being eclipsed by motorized traffic is a story paralleling the spread of affluence out into blue-collar districts after the wars. From being the exclusive purview of big business owners, cars became common possessions among working class men post-Second World War. Their new affluence afforded them cars, which in turn afforded them the opportunity to spread out and live in houses resembling those of the owning class too: detached ones, on miniature properties, each around a quarter acre in size. Any honest employee could now live as a gentleman, and dress like one too, as they travelled to work in the sheltered confines of a kind of machine their working class fathers could not have dreamed they would own.

By the 1970s, second-wave feminism was emboldening masses of women to copy what masses of men had copied from their middle class bosses. Their desire to drive created the two-car household and the double garage. The four-car garage followed when greater affluence still, in the 1980s, meant families could afford to let their young adult children in on the act of car ownership. No matter how inconvenient it may be to live on the back of a garage and to have to use a car just to buy a bottle of milk, it is worth it for the prestige. To live any other way would be to ignore the pride your grandparents would feel, had they lived to see all their descendants own their own cars.

## The Prestige
## Bicycle Market

Large sectors of the population reject the simple equation that cars equal status. Many see the value of owning fewer cars, but living closer to town. Then there is generation-Y, who Richard Florida argues are shunning cars altogether by moving to cities where they can live lives oriented around transit and cycling.

It is one thing, I would argue, to react against a visible sign of your parents' world view by not buying a car. It is another to shirk their unspoken creed. The Boomers and Silent Generation were incredibly earnest when it came to making major investments in wheels – with loans, insurance, Haynes manuals, etcetera – as though buying a car were an essential step towards fully fledged citizenry.

Is it so surprising then to find the new rise in cycling in car-loving nations coinciding with a spike in the sale of bikes that have price tags comparable to that of a car? Perfectly adequate commuting bikes can be 30 times cheaper than the kinds of pro-quality sports bikes many cyclists are buying, principally to use for commuting. However, a cheaper bike would not do for some people what a 10,000 or 15,000 euro bicycle can do for their status. A cheap bike does not achieve what that third or fourth garage door can achieve for the ego of someone whose pride is tied up with cars. Neither can cheap bikes satisfy the cultural expectation, in many corners, that one's mode of transport warrants a major financial outlay. Bicycling, for many, has become unnecessarily but delightfully pricey. In class terms a bicycle, for some people, is like a fifth family car, a must-have commodity if one is to keep on keeping up with the Joneses.

This effete and seemingly irrational dimension to contemporary cycling would understandably irritate many people with left or green leanings. They might agree to turn a blind eye though, if they were to carefully consider eventualities flowing from the treatment of cycling merely as a handmaiden to other political or ecological agendas instead of as something that each cyclist should be free to pursue as they please.

Consider a cycle-path advocate with a primary interest in public health and how they might react, for argument's sake, if they saw it was becoming trendy for cyclists to smoke. Never mind the freedom of movement cycling affords, they would prefer people take trains instead, where smoking is banned. Likewise, promoting cycling out of a concern for global warming rather than seeing green dividends as a bonus of cycling could see cycling being abandoned altogether if carbon-neutral cars came along.What of the transit engineer, who might want to triple the number of buses as an alternative way to deter driving? Such an approach would yield next to no public health benefits.

Of these four: (1) cycling for cycling's sake; (2) public health; (3) environmentalism; and (4) urban transit, it is only the first that, if pursued faithfully, would yield dividends for the remaining three interest groups. It follows that environmentalists, public health campaigners and transit planners would ultimately have their own interests served better if together they agreed to give pre-eminent regard to the needs of cycling, pursued with no extrinsic pressures.

What then of bicycling advocates whose interest in the subject follows on from their anti-consumerist stance? For this group as well, compromise would be strategic. Irritated though they may be that some cyclists were displaying their wealth through expensive cycling equipment, they would nonetheless be forced to accept that even the most wantonly equipped cyclist is consuming less with their hobby than they would if they were seeking their status with luxury cars. And, since cycling status cannot entirely be bought with equipment – just as intellectual status does not correlate directly to the size of one's library – consumerist cyclists deserve credit for at least pursuing a kind of snobbery for which the monetary costs are heavily subsidized, with physical fitness, some daring and skill. Add Marxists then to the list of stakeholders who stand to gain if they go along with cycling in all its diversity, rather than as they would ideally like cycling to be.

### Flows of Cultural Capital

Venturing from the dry land of empirical concerns about lane widths and volumes of traffic into the waters of class bought with prestigious possessions is to enter a realm in which architects swim every day.[1] The art of architecture is, often and undeniably, one of conferring users and patrons with status, not necessarily using marble and gold plated taps, but more often using modest materials handled with learning and moral integrity – the later approach starting with Bramante's Foundling Hospital in Florence, which he built from the cheapest grey stone, though with perfect proportions to reflect his high learning. Today, similarly, the world's tallest building (wherever it may be, on the week that you read this) will not be receiving so much attention in the architectural press. That will be going to something modest, and green, that only those with the requisite learning will be able to recognize for its worth.

Already architecture has started the job of lending cycling cache. Just as architecture did for Romans as they expanded their empire, or for the Medici's image in Florence, or as it is doing right now for Apple – whose flagship glass-fronted stores give consumers a sense they are buying more than an iPhone and MacBook, the sense that they belong to something much bigger – architecture is being used to raise the image of cycling. In the language of Pierre Bourdieu, architecture is lending to cycling some of its vast cultural capital. In turn architects are repaid by having the intangible qualities of cycling conferred on their buildings. Cycling speaks of

1
For an engaging, if bitter, explanation of architects' wielding of cultural capital in terms of Pierre Bourdieu's writings, see: Gary Stevens, The Favoured Circle, (Cambridge, MA: MIT Press, 2002).

<u>top left & right, middle</u>
Washington Bikestation,
Washington, DC
Photo: Steven Fleming

<u>bottom</u>
Monthly critical mass ride,
San Francisco
Photo: Steven Fleming

health and wellbeing, stoic resilience, frugality, concern for the planet, refined design, fearlessness, fairness: all qualities architects can badge themselves with the moment they design a building that celebrates bikes.

Ways cultural capital can be exchanged between the worlds of cycling and architecture are especially apparent in cities where people tend to commute a long way using expensive sports bicycles that they are not prepared to chain to street poles in front of their offices. By the time this book reaches the shelves, many sprawling cities where planners are aiming to increase rates of cycling will have at least one bicycle parking station that uses architecture to spread the message that cycling has status.

Our focus, right now, is not on cities in Northern Europe or Japan, where millions commute daily on lack-lustre bikes and where bicycle parking stations can be huge but unglamorous. Urban consolidation in these places means commuting distances are considerably shorter than in the sprawling cities of the New World. Cycling prevailed in most of these cities too because these cities are flat and thus able to be ridden on heavy steel bikes that are of little value to thieves. Most importantly, in these more mature cycling cities middle-class cyclists have no battle to wage against perceptions that only society's outcasts use bikes for getting around. Thus the norm in such places is for short, level rides made on sturdy but inconspicuous bikes. VMX Architects' bare bones, open-air bike parking station near Amsterdam's central train station is filled with 2,500 such bikes. While this building has been recognized in the architectural press, more of that fanfare concerned its scale and unusual function than its sophisticated architectural detailing or style. It was meant – though this has been forgotten – to be a temporary structure.

By contrast, KGP Design Studio's bike-transit centre in Washington, referred to in the last chapter, has as many panes of tempered glass and as many stainless steel spider clamps as any Apple store or state-owned museum – such elements being some of today's markers of architectural sophistication, the way pilasters on a Palazzo once were in Italy. Washington's Bikestation was not built to serve a demand, like a station in the Netherlands. It was built to create a demand. Its function is mostly symbolic. It was built to raise the profile of cycling in a sprawling car city, where it is assumed cyclists must share road space with drivers. Architectural symbols of power are conferred upon cyclists by proxy, hopefully so that drivers show them respect.

By Dutch standards the Washington Bikestation was hideously expensive, costing 3 million dollars while providing storage for less than 100 bicycles. However, the District of Columbia Department of Transportation, in funding this building, banked on converting more than 100 Washington drivers to cycling. Three million dollars was the cost of an architectural sign to the whole city that the district sanctions cycling. Authorities in Washington seem to have taken the view – though they may not have used the same terms – that expanding the empire of cycling in the USA requires more than simply an expansion of bicycle paths and the raising of public awareness. For the Romans, new roads and show-crucifixions were not enough either. Rome had to replicate its principal buildings throughout the occupied colonies before Rome's subjects believed it was in charge.

2
S. Peltzman, 'The Effects
of Automobile Safety
Regulation', *Journal of
Political Economy*, vol. 83
(1975) no. 4, 677-725.

3
Robert B. Noland, 'Per-
ceived Risk and Modal
Choice: Risk Compensa-
tion in Transportation
Systems', *Accident Analysis and Prevention*, vol. 27
(1995) no. 4, 503-521.

Likewise, claiming car dominated streets in the name of the bicycle would be helped along a good deal if architecture were added as a third prong.

The architect and cyclist in me have conflicting thoughts about this. My profession has me wanting to see architecture employed in a classical manner, as an expression of power. What bothers me as a cyclist is the political context that gives rise to such buildings as the Washington Bikestation. It is one that assumes cyclists will always ride on the road among cars, pleading for respect, yet knowing that even if respect comes they will come out the loser in any mishap.

Social scientists studying ways people change their behaviour depending on perceived risk speak of risk compensation – driving faster because you have been made to wear a seatbelt, for instance.[2] One researcher in the field, Robert Noland, looked at perceptions regarding improved conditions for cyclists and compared perceived improvements with increases in numbers of people commuting by bike.[3] He found that where a population perceived cycling to be, for example, 10 per cent safer due to some recent upgrade, there would not just be a 10 per cent increase in trips made by bike. Noland's surveys found a 1.19 magnitude, or 'elasticity factor', meaning a 10 per cent increase in perceived safety would lead to an 11.9 per cent increase in numbers of people commuting by bike. The danger, Noland warns, is that perceived safety and actual safety are not the same. A building that increases perceived safety by state-sanctioning cycling could simply be throwing the unwitting into a lion's den of deadly conditions out there on the streets.

Advocates for claiming cyclists' rights to the road don't drop their case there. Their argument is that louring more cyclists to battle will eventually see this war won. As with any war, some soldiers will die. The analogy between the Roman Empire's expansion and that of the empire of cycling remains true on many levels – at least among those choosing to fight for an expansion of cycle space on a battle field of drivers' choosing.

## Architecture and Empires

Legends of their might can blind us to the Romans' tenuous grip. At the apogee of the Pax Romana, 50 million people of various religions and races had acquiesced to be ruled over and pay taxes to just 4 million Romans. While most of those 50 million had learned from the death of their countrymen that Roman forces could crush any uprising despite those ten-to-one odds (just look at what happened to Boudicca!) fear alone does not account for so many internalizing the right to rule of so few. Fear does not explain why so many forsook their former religions, their identities, to become Roman soldiers and citizens if offered the chance. Monuments helped them towards their decisions.

The good news is that using architecture to influence public perceptions should be less of a task for those expanding the empire of cycling than it was for the Romans. Cyclists may sense resentment for occupying space that car drivers would say is exclusively theirs, but Rome and her puppet rulers had to deal with outright fear and loathing, not just petty resentment. And though Lycra attire can be provocative, signalling to drivers that cyclists plan to encroach on what they thought was their lane space, team kits are hardly as antagonistic as the uniforms Roman soldiers arrived in when they marched into new territories. And while cyclists may be an affront to some drivers' belief systems – their right to burn finite resources or their choice of big houses at the ends of long freeways – cyclists hardly have so much influence that drivers can worship no lord over Lance Armstrong, the way Rome's subjects put the emperor first. The cost for Rome, in architectural terms, would be acres of arcuated structures faced with Greek style columns and lintels lest they look crude and uncultured – the Romans were mortally afraid of being seen as just thugs. The architectural cost of raising the image of cycling in new cycling territories will be less than it was for that exemplary empire from whom we are taking some notes. The cost for the empire of cycling would be nearer to what Apple is spending on stores.

The bad news is that propagandizing for cycling on drivers' turf has not proven very effective thus far. On their turf, drivers at worst stand to lose a few minutes. Cyclists are risking their lives.

## Cycle Space: Where It Is Better to Ride Than to Walk

Before it is done with completely, the imperial analogy can give us some insights regarding which territories cycling might possibly conquer. Buildings that propagandize for cycling are not likely to be called for in far flung commuter suburbs, separated from major centres by long stretches of road on which only intrepid cyclists are likely to ride. If not forever damned, people who live in such places will at least be waiting some time before bicycling liberates them from their enslavement to cars. Their best hope is that rising energy prices will force all but human-powered and solar-powered vehicles off of the road. We could then see a rise in interest in velomobiles, a technology lying in wait for that day. But until then architects should not expect to see many commissions for bicycletecture coming from car land.

The contest for space by bicycling advocates is hardly likely to stop before all the world's central business districts are as safe for bicycling as they are for driving or walking. For those willing to risk it, cycling is already the fastest means of moving through cities. Given many cities were laid out assuming speeds of around 6 km/h – the surprisingly slow average speed of horse-drawn transportation – it could even be argued that cycling is too fast for cities, that if cyclists overran our old towns there would be crashes at every intersection. And there are indeed plenty of near misses at street corners in the old part of Amsterdam.

However, the greatest threat to cyclists in cities is cars. It is not until bicycling rates reach levels like those seen in Copenhagen, where hoards of cyclists are crushed into narrow bike lanes, that cyclists have an equal fear of each other. In cities where rates linger below 5 per cent, and where no one alive remembers a time when bicycling was a mainstream mode of getting around, reducing the threat to cyclists from cars to an acceptable rate is proving impossibly slow. Short of sending every driver back to be

## Velomobiles

Today's leading velomobile manufacturers (including Sunrider and Flevobike in the Netherlands and Trisled in Australia) have shifted their focus from human-powered land speed record attempts and are instead developing velomobiles to be driven/ridden on roads by commuters. These three-wheel recumbent bicycles with canoe-like casings to reduce wind drag and protect riders from rain can increase a rider's cruising speed on the flat by roughly a third, and allow them to reach frightening speeds when heading downhill. Riders in hilly cities often add electronic assist to their transmissions, as the pedalling position and extra weight of these bikes means they can be considerably slower uphill.

Velomobile enthusiasts report drivers give them more space on the road; we can assume most are aghast. They also enjoy commuting in their regular work clothes. Being enthusiasts, few confess to certain drawbacks: the lack of agility; claustrophobia and limited road viewing, especially in fully enclosed models; and the high price of those models people are first drawn to because they look sci-fi.

Manufacturers press on though, confident velomobiles will have their day when oil prices, or awareness of health or carbon emissions, thin the numbers of cars on the roads and velomobiles start taking their place. The makers listed above are among those building cheaper and more practical craft.

Images courtesy of Sunrider

license tested and at the same time installing segregated infrastructure everywhere, all in one hit, waiting for change to occur is unpromising. For the empire of cycling, universal and truly safe access will undoubtedly be the ultimate prize, if they are lucky enough to still be alive when it happens.

During the interim years we need to focus on the frontier lands for cycling in car cities, namely in the former industrial zones. Most cities have them: disused former industrial land parcels, mostly on level ground where once there were dockyards, canals, rail lines, rail shunting lines, factories, and so forth. Seen in isolation, they are great places for parks, modern offices, public buildings and medium- to high-density housing developments. But if viewed on a map, they generally link together in vast networks, having tendrils stretched over whole cities, perfect for cycling. The conversion of one kind of space – the rail lines – for bicycle use is being keenly watched by groups like Railtrails Australia and Rails-to-Trails in America. In the eyes of planners though, former slaughter yards, docklands, dumps and the likes have not stood out as being any more important to cyclists than anyone else with an interest in the release of new land.

This is not to say cycling is being neglected by those involved in master-planning this kind of land; most master plans, naturally, include shared cycle/pedestrian paths, stretching as far as can be conceived. The existence of many cycleway plans – whether extant or on paper – can be attributed to one very influential consultant, Jan Gehl, who remains an unwavering champion of bicycle transit. Lacking from the discourse though is a sense that cycling could well become the dominant mode of transportation for brownfield redevelopment areas, when the conversion of those sites is no longer a patchwork affair but absolute. New towns and parks, presently interspersed between sites still clinging to industrial functions, or areas awaiting funding to be converted are set to form contiguous networks, possibly as soon as the next peak in the development cycle. Rather than driving or bussing it to particular areas and then walking, any able bodied person would have little trouble riding all the way from their homes on what tend to be the most level parts of our cities.

One paradox is that in these areas where walkability is an espoused intension of planners, walking could soon be a casualty. Pedestrians outnumbered by cyclists, the latter having whole tracts opening to them, could be put off from walking in shared zones the way cyclists avoid using roads that have too many cars. And, feeling disempowered, more and more pedestrians are likely, in time, to get with the strength and start cycling too. They needn't be bullied to ride. They could be provided alternative paths where they could keep walking, paths that could be narrow and textured and therefore not appealing to cyclists, like the ones Dutch landscape architects West-8 have provided at Lincoln Park in Miami Beach, Florida.

Most design professionals will not be involved in planning for, or advocating, a takeover of walking by cycling; or, conversely, defending walking from such a hypothetical eventuality. Nor is it the role of this book to proselytize, either for or against bicycle domination, the relocation of industry or the conversion of car lanes to bike lanes. The aim rather is to alert architects, urban designers and planners to the likelihood of cycling rates snowballing, downtown and in post-industrial zones in particular,

4
*The Dream of the 90s*
is the theme song to
the IFC comedy series
*Portlandia*, which satirizes
various countercultures,
including bike messenger
culture, behind Portland's
GFC-defying renaissance.

and to be prepared. When design professionals are called on to creatively and meaningfully introduce buildings into areas where driving is frustrating, walking is slow and cycling is best, it will be advantageous if they can see the land they are developing as belonging to what growing numbers of people will be viewing as a part of their cycle space.

## Subcultures Relish
## at the Margins

Coining the term cycle space represents an interest in learning from a comparable term, queerspace. Popularized by Aaron Betsky as a way of theorizing architecture in areas colonized by homosexual communities, it offers useful parallels for those of us considering space now being colonized by those who ride bikes. Cyclists, it can be said, know something about feeling misunderstood, maligned and forced to claim space not freely given, all problems homosexuals know only too well. In the eyes of some drivers, cyclists are queer. We use critical mass rides the way homosexuals use gay pride parades, as a way of pleading for space in the city, and I believe we would be wise to take a cue from gay communities and congregate in certain parts of the city to escape prejudice.

Both terms, cycle space and queerspace, are unlikely to ever appear written on master plans, due to their being phenomenological constructs. To illustrate, a straight person could easily cross the same park every day of their life, unaware that it is a queer haunt, just as a non-cyclist could stroll along a foreshore promenade with cyclists whizzing both sides and have no idea they are walking on what to thousands of cyclists is a key transit corridor. You need to be queer to see queerspace. You need to ride to see cycle space.

Choosing a term that echoes Betsky's term queerspace also serves to remind architects that trend-setting minorities can trigger gentrification. And architects *love* gentrification: it brings them commissions. The story of homosexuals colonizing Manhattan's Meat Packing District in the 1970s, with nightclubs especially, is foundational to anyone in the field of queer studies. Four decades on, this former light industrial area is one of Manhattan's most expensive addresses, with signature buildings by Meier, Polshek, Nouvel and Gehry, and with the much lauded Highline terminating there in a crescendo. But the gay clubs moved north to Chelsea decades ago and with them a wave of gentrification is pushing further north still, into Hell's Kitchen. Queerspace is moving north along the west arm of the Hudson like a frontal weather system, raining hip buildings, both new and newly made-over.

At a time when property prices are in decline across the USA and people are moving back in with their folks, those parts of Portland, Oregon where the most people cycle are enjoying some of the lowest vacancy rates and buoyant property prices in the entire country. While some new arrivals in Portland may have been attracted to subcultures other than cycling or *The Dream of the 90s*,[4] there can be no denying safe cycling has been a big draw. It is entirely characteristic of bike lovers to choose where they live based on the safety of the bicycle transit. As a layer they might apply to maps when analysing sites in such areas the concept of a cycle space will help architects see otherwise nebulous patterns of behaviour affecting a site, and use that knowledge in considering the future life of their projects.

# Cycle

# Because

# It's

# FREE

# Singapore

What frightens me most about including a section on Singapore is not that I could find myself in a dissidents' cell on Sentosa next time I stop there, but that the People's Action Party (PAP) might actually implement some of my suggestions. They've already built a park I designed when I worked there in the mid-1990s (Serangoon Community Park), so maybe they would be hasty enough to build bicycle subways, as I'm about to suggest: two tunnels, one in each direction, letting cyclists make their own back drafts, following the course of their Mass Rapid Transit (MRT) lines and feeding into the underground shopping malls that cluster around most of the stations. Cyclists could fly around freely, out of the heat and tropical downpours – a brilliant suggestion, and with their resources and control of the media the PAP could implement it with the stroke of a pen. No community consultation required, just posters on buses telling their population how free and healthy transport has become theirs to enjoy.

The PAP (or 'Singapore Inc.' as many jokingly know it) has proven itself a consummate manager of a huge pension fund siphoning much of its citizens' earnings and returning them close to the rate of inflation. However, it is a regime that turns a buck from more than just pension funds. It also profits from transit. Subway stations are married to government-owned shopping arcades choked with commuters. To many locals these Piranesian labyrinths are more than just throughways. They are destinations in their own right, for a night on the town, exploring new underground eateries. If anyone finds

1
Estimates and figures taken from Singapore's Land and Transport Authority's website, One Motoring: http://www.onemotoring.com.sg/publish/onemotoring/en/lta_information_guidelines/buy_a_new_vehicle.html (accessed 16 March 2012).

their way to the surface they will find roads it is illegal for them to cross. They will be forcibly directed back underground, where shopkeepers pay the most rent.

If the government profits handsomely from users of public transport, it makes an absolute killing on drivers. On top of fuel taxes, high annual registration fees and congestion taxes, drivers pay import duties of 31 per cent, '*Additional Registration Fees*' of 140 per cent of the cost of their car, and must attach a Certificate of Entitlement (COE) to each car they wish to take on the road – the government sells ten-year CEOs, limited by a quota, to highest bidders for roughly 25,000 euro.[1] Encouraging the use of bicycles, which aren't easily taxed,

page 98
Waterfront urban renewal, Singapore
Photo: Steven Fleming

left
Waterfront/cycle-space architecture, Singapore
Photo: Steven Fleming

right
Underground Singapore
Photo: Steven Fleming

would impact the government's revenue base.

The government in Singapore boasts of a network of parkway connectors for cyclists; but like most bike path maps in the world, they describe a network that looks much better on paper than on the ground. On the ground it is characterized by impossible road crossings, 'cyclists dismount' signs and long stretches with no visual cues to tell riders they have not strayed.

The district of Tampines in the east of Singapore has been promoted by local government as a bike friendly town because cyclists there have been allowed to ride in pedestrian zones. But cyclists ride on footpaths all over Singapore. The only difference in Tampinese is police have been assigned to watch them more closely and fine anyone deemed to be reckless.

Regardless of public relations claims to the contrary, bicycle transit is stymied all over Singapore. Vehicular roads don't have safe shoulders. Bike paths are broken by every conceivable obstacle. Users of shared zones have no way to calculate

when and for what they might be fined. As if to protect the viability of the road and metro networks from which they profit, the government has a calculated stranglehold on pan-island cycling.

Nothing, however, will stop the Chinese or Indian populations from cycling around their local neighbourhoods. As happens in their ancestral homelands, people of Chinese and Indian decent fill their local streets here with the sounds of squeaky bike wheels and litter footpaths near local train stations with as many bikes as one would find littered near stations in the Netherlands. Neighbourhood cycling is deeply ingrained in these Asian cultures.

It is middle and longer distance cycling that is neglected. It is a pity that most Singaporeans do not even realize that with minimal fitness almost any of them could easily cycle across much of their tiny flat island in less time than it would take if they used public transport. Slowly though this seems to be changing.

I know from my own blogging that Singaporeans are engaged in web-based discussions about bicycle transit. I know from my blogging and on-the-ground observation that a disproportionately high number of those Singaporeans who share my passion are expatriates that have come to the island, bringing with them that Protestant habit of commuting all the way from home to the office. Not having been raised on

PAP propaganda – hailing the Mass Rapid Transit (MRT) as Lee Kuan Yew's gift to a nation – newcomers don't tolerate the mode change with the same acquiescence shown by most locals. Foreigners don't want to cycle to the station, chain up, swipe their card and then cram into a carriage just to travel 4 or 5 km to a nearby part of the same city. They want to ride their bikes the whole way.

The area around Robertson's Quay has long had a high concentration of *ang mos* (Malay for 'white ghosts', now a slightly endearing term for the Western expatriate). From Robertson's Quay it is a short bike ride, following a riverfront promenade where once there were docks, to the city. Increasingly, people living in this part of town are cycling along the river to work in the city, swapping congested roads and cramped public transport for a 10-minute ride, barely enough time to start sweating. The same humidity that makes walking uncomfortable in this tropical location helps to cool moving cyclists. Notwithstanding the presence of pedestrian-only underpasses and bridges, and some off-putting road crossings, a network of waterfront paths has the makings of a cycle-space route from Robertson's Quay all the way to the Bukit Timah Nature Reserve. Planners know the potential. They've drawn it on a map of parkway connectors. All that remains is for them to smooth the path to those connectors and to see those routes as real transit corridors, not just amenities for health and recreation.

The deal Confucius brokered between the Chinese and their emperors is that rulers should be allowed to get on with the business of ruling, while individuals focus on the health, wealth and wisdom of themselves and their families. Cycling improves people's health. It saves them money. It reduces time spent commuting and therefore increases time available for self-development, for example through education. It is only a matter of time before this country demands it.

# Chapter 5

# Aesthetic Directions for Cycle-Space Architecture

The kind of state that promotes cycling is the kind that promotes individual freedom. Cycling grants freedom of mobility to every age group, from children to the elderly, and across all social spectrums, from executives to complete non-participants in the economy. Susan B. Anthony's remark that the bicycle was the greatest ever tool in the emancipation of women has become a slogan for bicycle advocates. The same device that can keep pace with city traffic can be carried up stairs and ridden down hallways. Style wise, bikes can be worn in more ways than our hair. Given the way individualism is so intrinsic to bicycling, it would be natural if individual expression were seen as a hallmark of buildings in cycle space.

This chapter is directed towards designers who don't slavishly follow stylistic trends, but forge their own path, the way cyclists chart their own innovative routes through the city. I want to ground it in the thinking of art philosopher Arthur C. Danto, as he is a champion of individualism – or deep pluralism, as he would say – rather than the idea that artists (or architects, or urban designers) should all subscribe to the same manifestos.

Danto has a particularly useful way of defining an art object that is generally transferable to architecture too. He argues that artefacts become art when they are produced by the artist to be about something. His favourite illustration is Andy Warhol's work *Brillo Box*. Though the *Brillo Box* in the gallery looks exactly the same as a box of Brillo pads in the supermarket, the work of art is pregnant with meaning that the art world can recognize and be interested in. It invites them to ask: What is art, anyway?

According to this definition a work of architecture, as opposed to a run of the mill building, is one to which the architectural world naturally looks for some kind of meaning. This is an incredibly liberal and broad definition of architecture. A building can be about the idea of function, if function is presented in a way that invites us to think about functionalism. Yet a building needn't be self-consciously functionalist to be called architecture. Any of a number of competing streams of architectural thinking – semiotics, phenomenology, identity politics, expressionism, high-tech, and so forth – can elevate a building to the level of architecture by inviting those with an interest in the world of architecture to engage with that building's meaning.

It isn't for me to say what deeper meanings should preoccupy architects building on bicycling turf. What I can say is that meaningfulness, of whatever kind, is worth thinking of as the *sine qua non* of a building if we are to agree it has architectural substance. This broad and accommodating definition of architecture means I can put forward the widest range of agendas for architects to take up, if they like. There must be dozens more. Those outlined below are limited – severely, I fear – by my own imagination. Think of them as examples of the kinds of conversations architects might engage with to make their buildings meaningful, and therefore architectural, where clients or their public are as excited about cycling as their grandparents were about driving.

Renowned architecture historian of the mid-twentieth century Nikolaus Pevsner once said that a bicycle shed is not architecture, Lincoln Cathedral is architecture.[1] He was half right: most bike sheds are devoid of meaning, where clearly cathedrals are brimming. It was Pevsner's

1
Nikolaus Pevsner, *An Outline of European Architecture*, 6th ed. (Harmondsworth, UK: Penguin Books, 1960), 7.

2
Reyner Banham, 'A Black Box: The Secret Profession of Architecture', *New Statesman and Society*, 12 October 1990, 22-25.

3
Hiroyuki Suzuki and Shuhei Endo, *Shuhei Endo: Paramodern Architecture*, edited by Hiroyuki Suzuki, translated by Richard Sadleir (Milan: Electa Architecture, 2003); the shed was built in Maihara-cho, Shigan in 1993-1994.

one-time student Reyner Banham who picked up on the sense in which Pevsner was wrong: 'This was not only a piece of academic snobbery that can only offend a committed cyclist like myself, but also involves a supposition about sheds that is so sweeping as to be almost racist.'[2]

Pevsner could have picked any other kind of shed as his canard and probably have elicited no reaction at all from Reyner Banham. However, Banham was a keen cyclist (as we'll see later in this chapter) and was therefore understandably sensitive. Most cyclists are. We object to anything that belittles this proud yet vulnerable mode of transportation we use. If a building for bikes must be a shed, to save money, then may it at least be a bike shed like the one on the cover of architect Shuhei Endo's monograph *Shuhei Endo: Paramodern Architecture*,[3] with corrugated iron and cold-formed steel sections twisted in ways that recall Möbius strips, and therefore speak to conversations in architectural circles. That at least is an *architectural* bike shed.

It would be better still if buildings in cycle space spoke to architectural conversations that somehow involved bikes. Each of the passages in this chapter announces one such conversation.

### Off the Shelf,
### Yet Perfectly Fitting

Assembly-line car manufacturing has stimulated architectural thinking before, so it seems fair to ask if the way bikes are manufactured should not inspire architects working in cycle space. A particularly relevant parallel can be drawn between ways the bicycling industry – and architects – deal with standardized systems, outsourcing and the limits of designers' volition.

It has become rare to find a vertically integrated company in charge of every stage of a bicycle's production. In its heyday Raleigh designed and manufactured almost every component going onto its bicycles. Today the word Raleigh still evokes the former glory days of British manufacturing, but it no longer stands for one factory in England embossing the letter R on the end of each nut.

The enormity of the bicycle industry and the nature of a bicycle being an assemblage of separate components has allowed outsourcing to be taken to extreme ends. Some of the mass-market brands with which we are most familiar can place orders with assembly plants that in turn order frames, brakes, hubs and gears from other specialist manufacturers, who themselves buy minor components from yet others. The general flattening of the industry's structure has seen many axle widths, wheel sizes, bearing cup diameters, etcetera become rare items. The 28-in wheels Britain once used for its roadsters, for example, are now special orders in many countries. Manufacturers with little control over their supply chains naturally favour standard-gauge parts that can be substituted for parts from any supplier; thus they prefer 700-c or 26-in wheels, the two most common sizes. There are still a few somewhat vertically integrated companies, Brompton for instance, with its highly specialized folding bikes, unique gears and Brompton-specific components. However, such makers are at the margins. Overwhelmingly, bicycles with different brand names are becoming more alike every year.

One site of resistance to bicycle sameness is the annual North American Handmade Bicycle Show (NAHBS), where boutique bike makers showcase their craftsmanship and innovations. From baroque lug work to minimalist bikes seemingly forged from single blocks of titanium, the show provides thousands of aficionados with a chance to meet and celebrate an enormous variety of bicycle designs. Yet even here there are no makers of complete bicycles. There are parts suppliers – both mass market and boutique – and there are makers of frames who put whole bikes together using others' components. Add to that the capability of interchanging boutique components with mass-market equivalents from big players like Shimano and SRAM, and you have an industry where standardization and customization slide to and fro. In the building industry such levels of seamless interchangeability remain largely illusive.

Many architects have as their heroes such old masters as Frank Lloyd Wright, who would personally design the furniture for each of his houses, or Louis I. Kahn, who would lovingly detail exposed structural concrete as if it were marble. However, the rise of design and construct (D&C) contracts and of specialist project management companies has relegated many architects to a less volitional role. They find themselves beholden to builders and designing on the fly, in many cases.

Depending on how they look at the subject, architects casting their eye to the bicycle industry because it seems to be making good use of mass-produced components could find cause for hope, or despair. They would certainly despair at interface problems when they do still occur.

NAHBS though represents a triumph of horizontally integrated design and manufacturing. It shows designers can take the best from the worlds of bespoke making and mass-production, as long as they have a mastery of the way various component and frame configurations all interface. If we think of a building's structural frame as something analogous to a bicycle's frame, then look at the custom bike scene, we can imagine every building having its own unique and perhaps highly articulated structure – a structure that has been modulated in such a way as to give the architects and builders the widest possible range of cladding and glazing systems from which to choose.

Standardization, modulation and outsourcing: none of these are new concepts in building. The Harappan civilization employed standard-size bricks 5,000 years ago, across the whole Indus Valley. Modernist architects loved the idea of building from off-the-shelf parts, as Charles and Ray Eames did to aplomb with their Case Study House No. 8 (Los Angeles, 1949). However, in a technological age with global trade networks the potential is greater. If industry-wide conventions and modules can ensure they will have exposure to the widest possible markets, manufacturers can recoup R&D and tooling costs associated with developing new building systems. And if architects subscribe to consensuses they can avail themselves of the fruits of manufacturer's R&D, even when late changes are foisted upon them. Late in the piece they can go with the cheapest or best, as easily as swapping one brand of handlebar for another.

<u>top</u>
Reyner Banham riding his
Moulton F-frame bicycle in
London,1964
Source: Reyner Banham,
*Design by Choice* (New
York: Rizzoli, 1981)

<u>left</u>
Norman Foster hugging
his Moulton space-frame
bicycle
Photo: Patrick Lichfield
Courtesy of Foster +
Partners

<u>bottom</u>
Steven K. Roberts with his
'gizmo logically-intensive'
recumbent bicycle
Courtesy of Nomadic
Research Labs photo
archives

The proposition is that architects taking inspiration from bicycles could revive the fascination with mass production that architects developed during the machine age. The dream of mass production has been pursued since Joseph Paxton had the parts of Crystal Palace in London (1851) made elsewhere and then assembled on site. Le Corbusier tried it with his Citrohan House, which was to include as many off-the-shelf parts as could be sourced. Japanese Metabolists took the analogy with car making as far as they could, imagining living units being prefabricated and plugged into lift cores like assembly-line produced cars parked in the sky. The kit-of-parts doctrine of high-tech architects is in this vein as well. Although we must not forget a competing architectural agenda – using computer aided manufacturing (CAM) to build non-linear forms – bicycles can inspire us by the way standardized parts are utilized in their production; in any case non-linear buildings like Frank Gehry's Bilbao, or LAB's Federation Square, do use standard parts in their making, though cut to unique lengths and fixed at unique angles to make irregular shapes.

### Emulating Bicycles

There must be dozens of ways architects working in cycle space could take inspiration from bicycle frames. View a bike frame from behind, at an oblique angle, and you will see it is as complex in three dimensions as any of the non-orthogonal buildings to wow us since the advent of CAM. Can architects pursuing this kind of architecture learn from the way bike frames are made, with ultimate lightness and strength?

The façade for LAB's Federation Square in Melbourne was developed in collaboration with specialist architects Newtecnic in London. Rotating joints inspired by car tow balls connect regular steel sections at irregular angles.[4] Mero balls – steel balls typically with 12 threaded holes to receive dowels – might have provided a more elegant joint, but proprietary elements like these (Nodus balls and extruded hubs are two more) are made to join members at the regular angles corresponding to tetrahedral and other platonic solids, on which space frames and geodesic domes are normally based. When it comes to joining many struts approaching one fixing point, all from odd angles, no coupling system has yet been devised that is elegant enough to warrant adoption en masse as a building industry standard.

Bicycle-frame makers have traditionally joined tubes at odd angles using steel lugs. Custom bike makers demand an astonishing range of variants too, to accommodate the unique frame geometries that individual riders require. Keeping in mind that bicycle frames are not planar (the rear triangles flare to receive the rear wheel), and looking at the complexity of something like a bottom bracket shell, which receives the down tube, seat tube and both of the chain stays, we might take inspiration from bicycle lugs in developing more elegant joints for non-linear space frames. The tubular steel lattice covering the field in front of Frank Gehry's Jay Pritzker Pavilion in Chicago hints at the refined aesthetic that might be achieved.

The persistent appeal of lugged frames serves to remind us as well of the way articulated joints, be they on bicycle frames or on buildings, are pleasing to many viewers. Builders of every period have taken the meet-

4
See http://www.new-tecnic.com/projects/fed_sq.html (accessed 28 March 2011).

ing of column and lintel as an occasion not only for reinforcement, but articulation and decoration. Egyptian lotus bud and lotus leaf capitols; the Doric, Ionic and Corinthian capitols of the classical tradition; Buddhist and Hindu variants of classical capitols; the dougongs used in Chinese architecture to transfer roof and eave loads onto capitols: all these betray a seemingly innate impulse to provide visual interest wherever structural elements need to be joined. That we see lugged frame construction still being used to make the most prestigious bicycles, despite the advent of lighter techniques – TIG welded titanium and monocoque carbon fibre for instance – suggests the impulse is deeply ingrained, if not universal.

While we would not expect any bike loving architects to actually build using decorative lug work, the example is raised that we may be alive to the influence of bicycle design upon architecture. Already we have the story of Marcel Breuer admiring the curved handlebars of his Adler bicycle, then using similar bent steel in the design of his Wassily chair. Seeking a similar aesthetic and also wanting the strength and low weight of a bicycle, Charlotte Perriand turned to lengths of bicycle frame tubing to realize her famous Chaise Lounge. It can also be observed that Norman Foster's cherished Moulton space-frame bicycle looks unnervingly like many of his own buildings, for example the roof top element of Deutsche Bank Place, his building in Sydney. It should not come as a surprise in an age during which bicycles are being thought of as key to the future lives of our cities if solutions to problems in bicycle design inspire solutions to architectural problems even more often than they have done in the past.

One of the most commented upon attractions of cycling, particularly, it is said, among middle-aged men, is the opportunity cycling affords many of us of average means to own and tinker with sporting equipment surpassing Formula-1 cars in the quality of materials and levels of R&D invested in their making and their design. The most expensive bikes are those where virtually no part is made from any material other than carbon fibre or titanium, the two lightest materials for their relative strength that can be used in a bicycle. As both materials come down in price we are likely to see them being used more in buildings.

### The Allure of
### Platonic Ideals

Whether they are made from carbon fibre, TIG welded titanium or lugged and braised steel, most bicycles have frames built around a front and rear triangle, making a diamond shape. It is a configuration that in many ways seems self-evident and irreducible. It has certainly survived the test of time, having been used since 'safety bicycles' first appeared in the late 1800s. Its endurance for over a century and its relative complexity (frame, fork, wheels, transmission, handlebars and seat position all predetermined) makes the diamond frame bicycle a natural case in point whenever discussions arise among designers about the existence of archetypes.

This is a way of thinking about the design of functional objects that has been with us since the fifth century BC, when Plato introduced his theory of Forms, or Ideas. According to this theory the many things we see around us and call chairs, for example, are meant to participate in the invisible Idea of *The Chair Itself*. Anything that is hot is in fact participating in some Idea of absolute hotness, or *Hotness Itself*, which paradoxically doesn't produce heat we can feel. The Forms are intelligible, but cannot be sensed. Particular things are able to be sensed, but according to Plato's theory of Forms are unintelligible.

In architecture we see Platonic distinctions between Ideas and their earthly manifestations in French Enlightenment theorist Quatremère de Quincy's theory of types and Italian neo-rationalist Aldo Rossi's argument that all the world's buildings of a particular type could be studied to reveal the essence of House, Prison, and so on.

The theory is also echoed in various speeches and essays by American architect Louis I. Kahn, who saw a difference between the underlying 'form' corresponding to various building types and particular manifestations of those types, which Kahn called 'designs'. The sanctuary of his First Unitarian Church and School in Rochester, New York is surrounded by classrooms because Kahn believed the underlying (Platonic) 'form' of any such building had to be annular, just as a spoon must have a container and an arm to be called a spoon. Kahn spoke of spoons all needing this form, whether they be made of metal or wood, and whether they be shallow or deep. He might well have used the diamond-shaped bicycle as his illustration. It is one of the best examples of a design essence we know of that cannot be changed without making it worse. At least that is what many people believe.

In an article he wrote in 1960 about his beloved F-Frame Moulton bicycle, architecture critic and theorist Reyner Banham dismissed as nonsense all such theories of 'permanent and definitive forms'.[5] His bicycle did not have the diamond frame so many claimed to be absolute, yet as far as Banham could tell it performed even better. In the next seven years a string of speed records would be broken by riders on Moulton F-frames,[6] confirming Banham's hunch that the diamond belonged to a period in history and that there are no archetypal forms upon which buildings of the same type need to be modelled.

If it were true that the diamond frame could not be reduced without compromising speed, strength or weight, then rhetoric referring to Platonic ideals would be more convincing. However, the Moulton would not be the last unconventional bike to outperform its diamond-shaped cousins. By the late 1980s, medal sweeps by cyclists on RMIT Super Bikes and Lotus 108s prompted cycling's regulating body, the UCI, to rule that all riders compete on traditional diamond-shaped frames. The aim was to make the sport a competition between riders, not countries with huge R&D funds. Item 1.3.020 of the UCI's technical regulations states: 'The frame of the bicycle shall be of a traditional pattern, for example built around a main triangle.'[7] Additional clauses govern minimum and maximum dimensions in such a way as to sanction the diamond frame, at least until those rules are revoked, which doesn't seem likely in the foreseeable future. If the ruling were to be dropped tomorrow, top tubes and seat stays would almost certainly disappear altogether from road and track racing and bulbous, monocoque carbon frames would take over.

5
Reyner Banham, 'A Grid on Two Farthings', *New Statesman and Society*, 1 November 1963.

6
See http://www.moulton-bicycles.co.uk/heritage.html#recordsracing (accessed 31 March 2011).

7
See http://www.cycling.org.au/?MenuID=About+Us%2F20015%2F0&Page=8350 (accessed 30 March 2011)

8
Rudloph Wittkower,
*Architectural Principles in
the Age of Humanism* (New
York: W.W. Norton, 1971).

9
Aldo Rossi, *The Architec-
ture of the City*, translated
by Diane Ghirardo and
Joan Ockman (Cambridge,
MA: MIT Press, 1984).
First published in 1966 as
*L'architettura della città*.

10
Anthony Vidler, 'The Third
Typology', in: Kate Nesbitt
(ed.), *Theorizing a New
Agenda for Architecture:
An Anthology of Architec-
tural Theory 1965-1995*
(New York: Princeton
Architectural Press,
1996), 260-263.

But details of the UCIs rules are not widely known. Indeed, many ama-
teur bike racers would be surprised to learn they have spent thousands
of euros on frames shaped as they are just so that poor countries and
riders can have a sporting chance to compete. If they did know, fewer
would spend money on their equipment as though no price limit should
be placed on the thrill of going as fast as humanly possible. And if many
avid cyclists can hold onto the belief that diamond frames cannot be
surpassed, we can hardly expect this particular myth of Platonism's proof
to disappear from the design world any time soon. If anything, an age in
which cycling increasingly comes to emblemize health, environmentalism
and social equality will see even more architects saying their buildings
are timeless, just like diamond shaped bicycles.

## Making the City Your Office and
## the Whole World Your Home

Next are personal meditations of mine that come from spending an inordi-
nate portion of my life reading architecture theory and riding bikes. It has
occurred to me while riding, fielding work related phone calls, then stopping to attend to emails using my phone while wearing a waterproof jacket,
that I can make a city feel like my office. Actually, because bikes are so fast
I can make a city feel like a big building. Thanks to the leverage a bicycle
gives to each of my strides, I sometimes have a feeling of walking, only with
very long steps. If two walking paces take me 1 m, and two downward pedal
strokes propel me by 5 m, a city can feel as though it is five times smaller
by length, and 25 times smaller in terms of its area. I suspect people who
field work calls while driving are less astute to this shrinking, because: 1)
they are cocooned, 2) an accelerator pedal doesn't give the same feedback
you get from the physical world that you feel when you step on a bicycle
pedal, and 3) drivers have to keep stopping while cyclists roll on, which
makes cycling feel free the way walking feels free.

Books on the history of architecture often use the words microcosm
and macrocosm to describe ways architects have traditionally imagined
buildings as miniature versions of much bigger things. In the Renaissance,
the macrocosm architects thought of was Heaven. Rudloph Wittkower
describes Brunelleschi's circular church plans in this way.[8]

Today, if architects are going to conceive their buildings as miniature
versions of much bigger things, they will more likely imagine them being
miniature cities. One of the first texts to elevate the city in such a way
that architects might begin to see it as a macrocosmic model for buildings
was Aldo Rossi's *L'architettura della città*.[9] Architecture theorist Anthony
Vidler would call the European city a new article of faith for Rossi and
architects to come after, like Leon Krier.[10]

The analogy works in reverse too. In the years immediately following
Aldo Rossi's seminal text, the members of the Italian group Superstudio
were doing the opposite, conceiving not only cities but the face of the globe
as a single building. Although they have since claimed they were satirizing
modernism, the films and graphics they produced of their Continuous Monuments had a polemical, not a satirical tone. We get the impression that,

given the chance, they would have gone ahead with their proposal to build a never-ending access-floor made of white tiles that could be lifted to reveal all the services anyone would need to sustain life. It was never quite clear where people would shelter, go to the toilet or eat, but details like those are never at the forefront of fantasies of technologically enabled nomadism.

In 1983 a freelance writer on computer technology and avid adventure cyclists, Steven K. Roberts, began a 27,360-km broken journey around North America, on ever more 'gizmo logically-intensive' recumbent bicycles, which he built for himself between stages.[11] It was no more evident in Roberts's case than in Superstudio's how toileting and sheltering would be taken care of. He was more concerned with telling audiences how he typed his computer articles as he peddled, in binary, with keys beneath each of his handgrips, glancing between the road ahead and LCD screens behind his front fairing. He tells of residing – not on his bike, in hotel rooms or on a moving point on the map, but inside computer networks, a place that today we call cyberspace.

Three decades on, any cyclist with a voice recognition app on their smart phone could finish more typing and more business just riding around on a 6-kg track bike than Roberts could have achieved on his 125-kg rig. With an augmented reality (AR) app on their phone and perhaps satellite navigation, techno savvy cyclists could physically inhabit unfamiliar reaches of any city, as though they were locals. And while they ride, they could be texting, emailing, video-conferencing and in a limited way browsing the web, thereby psychologically inhabiting cyberspace, although they are physically cycling.

Now consider that, time wise, nothing makes a city smaller than a bicycle can – which is why businesses hire bicycle couriers when they want to transfer packages between opposite ends of crowded cities. A cyclist can cross town in the time it might take to walk between two anchor stores in a large shopping mall. Time wise, their bicycles shrink cities to the size of large buildings. While researching this book I had a chance encounter with Kevin (Squid) Bolger, a minor celebrity bike messenger in New York. It is ten minutes by bike from Mid Town to Greenwich, he told me. Lacking his experience, it took me two minutes longer.

Most bicycle couriers, as well as many other urban cyclists with nerve, ride fixed gear bikes that heighten the sense I described of pedal strokes feeling like levered up strides. Practiced riders can even stride backwards. A rider can't freewheel on these bikes, but then neither is it possible on foot to take a few brisk steps and then hope to glide. So our bicycle courier's cross-town jaunt is, in some sense, like a brisk walk, only his strides have been converted into the rotations of his rear wheel. With their dispatcher talking to them through an earpiece as though they were in the next room, and AR apps overlaying smart-phone screens with carefully edited data, bicycle messengers can further make the city feel like a building by stripping it of extraneous detail. Having scaled up their strides and tuned out the static, they are apprehending the city as though it were a building; the macro as though it was micro.

I spent a few days cycling willy-nilly around New York with this analogy in mind. Perceptually, could a bike make New York feel like a building? In

11
Steven K. Roberts,
*Computing Across
America: The Bicycle
Odyssey of a High-Tech
Nomad* (Medford, NJ:
Information Today, 1988).

honesty, I could not say my bike shrunk the city to the size of an apartment building. Popping back to the Meat Packing District from Midtown to pick up my jumper was somewhat more involved then backtracking the length of a corridor. I would say my bike shrunk New York to something the size of a mega-mall. Still, a mega-mall is a building.

As increasing numbers of theoretically minded architects engage with AR, during this period of intense interest in bikes the prospect of using the two to invert the microcosm/macrocosm equation – to see cities as buildings, not buildings as cities – could be a catalyst for investigations compared to which Superstudio's vision of people roaming a field of white tiles will look rather pedestrian (pun intended).

One such investigation is the Copenhagen Wheel, an e-assist bicycle hub with regenerative braking being developed by a team based at MIT, headed by Italian architect Carlo Ratti. The hub is controlled from and sends data to an iPhone in a handlebar mount. If many cyclists in the one city all used these hubs, apps on their iPhones could dynamically map data, such as pollution in various parts of the city, in that case helping riders choose cleaner routes. The hub is not yet commercially available and most likely will never catch on – prototypes weigh more than most bikes! But that won't stop architects dreaming of ways AR and the bicycle as a prosthesis can together transform our understanding of cities – these things we look to for authority the way former generations of architects looked towards heaven.

### More Reflections on
### Bicycles as Prostheses

The world of cycling can be very staid. Sports cycling is an odd fusion of backward looking UCI rules (outlawing sub 6.9-kg bikes, for example) and weekend competitors' own doubting of anything not used by pro teams; they forget, of course, that elite riders don't necessarily use the fastest equipment, but that which is pushed on them by sponsors. At the same time fashion-conscious cyclists, for whom living green can be just another manifestation of a highly attuned fashion sense, have shown a penchant for old bikes and therefore an even greater reluctance to embrace innovation in bike design; they would rather ride something predating derailers. As for infrastructure designers, just rolling out a curb detail copied from the Netherlands can have them hopping as though they've invented the wheel.

Contrasting the cycling world's conservatism, architecture theory often deals with the implications of technologies that may never impact our daily lives. Robotic prostheses, virtual reality, augmented reality, artificial intelligence, the idea that our children might become cyborgs: architecture theory engages with themes that many engineers in the bicycling world – whether at the sports end or transit end – would simply find irritating. Should we adjust, then, to a dearth of imagination on their part? Probably not.

Architectural educator and theorist Mark Wiggly has described the discipline of architecture as a kind of black sheep within universities, but one that nonetheless fulfils a deficiency within those institutions. 'On the one hand, the [final year thesis project] could not be more foreign to the university. But, on the other hand, its public oral defence by the student is the most faithful maintenance of the oldest and most central institution of the university.'[12] Having explored every vaguely related use of the word prosthesis, from the building being a prosthesis unto the body, to Freud's idea that our very consciousness is a prosthetic appendage on the body as well,[13] Wiggly argues that universities need schools of architecture the way a one-legged man needs his fake leg. I would argue the bicycle world has a missing leg too, for which the architectural imagination, looking as it does for left-of-field answers and backing these with sophistry, rhetoric and sometimes even sound logic, could be a prosthesis.

These imaginations of ours could run a long way with analogies concerning prostheses. They could really run wild with ideas flowing from a new concept-bike recently unveiled by Toyota[14] that allows riders to change gears just by thinking. The bike is called the PXP and comes with a helmet that conceals electroencephalography (EEG) electrodes, reading the rider's telepathic directions to their derailer to change gears up or down. Could EEG sensors in our helmets allow us to tell traffic lights that we want to turn left? Could we open doors with our minds, then ride through them? Could we relay messages to car driver's dashboards, alerting them to our presence? Could we answer our phones without touching a button? Could the gear levers on bikes, since we would no longer need them, be used to type?

The ability to control household appliances never quite justified the attachment of electrodes to the insides of our night caps, let alone surgically insert computer chips into our bodies. Why bother, when we can just use our hands? But in situations where our hands are engaged – because we are controlling a bike, for example – such powers could make a huge difference, allowing cyclists to control physical and virtual environments without losing balance or having to stop.

But the architectural imagination doesn't stop there. As John Ruskin argued, an architect stands apart from a good contract manager, detailer and supervisor of building construction as one who is able to 'tell us a fairy tale out of his head'.[15] How then might cities adapt to the needs of a bicycle born population that has cyborg powers? Undoubtedly we would colonize virtual realms. Already cyclists use their GPS units (in smart phones and cycle computers) to contribute to data pools like bikely.com, a crowd sourced repository of touring and training routes, mainly. Various platforms already exist for cyclists to train and even compete in real-time virtual environments, with their bikes attached to training machines that measure their wattage. One can imagine future versions of these being optimized to make use of inputs from EEG sensors and virtual reality hardware. As dizzying as bicycling phone apps already may seem, leading new apps might be precipitous of delusions of grandeur, when cyclists can use them to relay commands to machines simply by thinking.

However, the exploration of extreme boundaries would ideally be continued by avant-garde architects and students of architecture, rather than by career academics like me. I am alluding to experiments of the mind, like MVRDV's projections of cities if cars could fly, bicycle counter parts to which academics are best placed to reflect upon and critique.[16]

12
Mark Wigley, 'Prosthetic Theory: The Disciplining of Architecture', *Assemblage* (1991) no. 15 , 6-29.

13
Sigmund Freud, 'Metapsychological Supplement to the Theory of Dreams' (1916), in: *General Psychological Theory* (New York: Macmillan, 1963), 151.

14
Toyota's partners are an advertising company, Saatchi & Saatchi LA, online promoters Deeplocal, and bike brand Parlee Cycles.

15
John Ruskin, Lecture IV, 'The Influence of Imagination in Architecture', in: *The Two Paths: Being lectures on art and its application to decoration and manufacture*, delivered in 1858-1859 (London: G. Allen, 1906).

16
Winy Maas and Grace La (eds.), *Skycar City: A Pre-emptive History* (Barcelona: Actar, 2007).

# Cycle

## Because

# It's

## COOL

## Portland

Portland, Oregon is creating bike culture the way Los Angeles created car culture. But where LA gave us drive-in cafés with styling copied from car grills, twenty-somethings in Portland are congregating in brew pubs and cafés with names worth tattooing, like the Hopworks Bikebar, the Lucky Lab and Stump Town Café. Hopworks has hundreds of bike frames on display over the bar and old dragster bike seats for the intoxicated to rest their heads upon while they urinate. Walking along the bike racks outside of the Apex Bar is like walking through a custom bike show. The young are matching bar tape to their saddles as thoughtfully as young people elsewhere might match their shoes to their jeans. Track bars from the 1980s matched with cranks from the 1990s, or any other syntactical gaff, could undo a month's worth of networking. Don't think about coming here with a backpack. You must carry your purse in a messenger bag. Cruising around the Hawthorne district in the southeast part of town, anyone with an eye for bike culture would be struck by just how convincingly hundreds of people have made themselves look as though they work full time riding bikes, delivering parcels. Surely most of those kinds of jobs died with the advent of e-mail?

But this is a city of half a million people, where, on a good day, as many as 50,000 bikes will hit the street. Only a few riders need to be dreaming they're bike messengers for an outsider to gain the impression that all of Portland is faking.
A more balanced picture emerges out on the major bike routes flanking both sides of the river. Regular people on nondescript

bikes ride 8 and 16 km to work beside rivers and wetlands, in preference to driving. They are Portland's silent cycling majority.

Naturally people ask how an American city of just over 500,000 people could have so many people riding to work. The question is doubly puzzling when you consider the city's cold, rainy weather and hilly terrain. Cyclists I've spoken to here can only agree that there are many factors at play, among which the lifting bridges stand out.

Portland has five lifting bridges that are each raised a few times per day. When they're raised, cars are backed up for miles. Cyclists, of course, ride ahead to the boom gates. Then, when a bridge is lowered, the bike riders race ahead of all but the first few cars in the queue. This visible reminder that bikes are quicker cannot be dismissed as a factor in Portland's bike share. No commuter wants to be a regular loser in the race to and from work; and how much more gratifying it is to beat the herd via the less travelled road.

In a sense Portland itself is a less travelled road. Its gentrified Southeast district has more permaculture gardens than lawns. Restaurants and bars sell more fancy beer than fancy wine. Outside of Belgium, Portland has the largest cycle-cross scene in the world. Its second stadium was built for soccer, not American football. When members of the American Institute of Architects were threatening to walk, saying Michael Grave's winning design for the city administration building wasn't real architecture, but some kind of abomination, residents warmed to Grave's design – if wedding cake classicism was annoying to people in the rest of America, then obviously it was the right choice of style for their city. Portland's lead role in

page 118
Jonathan Maus of Bike-
Portland and Portland's
Bike Coordinator, Roger
Geller, Portland, OR
Photo: Michael
Colville-Andersen

left
Hopworks Bike Bar,
Portland, OR
Photo: Steven Fleming

right
Marsicek/Roberts House,
Portland, OR
Photo: Steven Fleming

cycling clearly fits with a broader narrative of differentiation from mainstream America.

A word of caution though: attributing high rates of bicycle commuting to Portland's alternative image trivializes generations of informed leadership, both in city hall and at grassroots level. Portland's now palpable civitas began with a movement to relocate the part of the US Route 99W then called Harbor Drive from the river alongside the downtown area to the outskirts of town. In effect, the town asked to be bypassed, forsaking the opportunity to serve weary drivers on the main road between Canada and California. Taken in the 1960s, that decision was clearly indebted to the grassroots movement led by Jane Jacobs on the East Coast that spared Greenwich Village being severed by the kind of highway Portland residents now wanted gone.

Harbor Drive was pulled up in the 1970s, leaving a fully realized stretch of cycle space in its wake, now called Tom McCall Waterfront Park. For cyclists who would prefer to dodge joggers

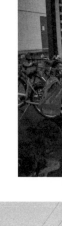

and dogs on long leads than be dodged themselves by cars and trucks, an unprecedented cycle-space zone came early to Portland, giving safe all-weather bicycle transport a foothold.

Three decades later, the impact is reflected in the way Portland builds. Enough home buyers come to Portland looking for a suburban life with no car that one local real estate agent named Kirstin Kaufman arranges regular open-house bicycle tours. She specializes in homes with no parking – except for bikes.

Local architects Jennifer Marsicek and Jason Roberts are completely tuned in to this bicycle-oriented take on the suburbs. When renovating their house they added a bike parking garage, complete with a bicycle-width automatic roller door entrance. That, plus a bike wheeling channel alongside a half flight of stairs to the basement, allows the family to come and go on their bikes in all weather without inconvenience. These features only added around 1,000 euros to the total cost of the project – roughly the price of a bike.

At the work-end of bike trips, the thinking is similar. Without wheeling channels on stairs leading to secure indoor bike parking, and lockers and showers, managers of commercial buildings have trouble leasing their office space. Recent upgrades to the Spalding Building downtown saw a ground floor bank safe turned into what could be the world's most secure bike room, with enormous safe doors and bikes hanging inside as though they were ingots of gold. This is a high-grade office building with no car parking – not even for CEOs – but luxurious locker and shower rooms. CEOs come to work here on bikes.

Bike storerooms in houses are commonplace throughout the Netherlands, and none of the road markings that Portland's Department of Transport have put down to help cyclists

hold a candle to an average curb treatment in Denmark. What is remarkable here is the overcoming of seemingly insurmountable barriers. Far more people regularly drive than ride bikes in Portland, yet biking has been influencing developers, planners and politicians. Cyclists are a minority, relegated to select streets, waterfronts and rail easements to minimize their impact on voters who drive, yet they are able to create their own haunts and even whole neighbourhoods completely invested in cycling. Some, we suspect, would go back to driving if cycling ever did take over the city and became truly mainstream – although the tattoo of a bike on their leg might be problematic.

# Chapter 6

# If Architects Designed Bicycle Transit

## Architects Focus
## on Aspirations

Whenever I buy a new bike it lives in my bedroom for at least a few weeks. I fetishize each component by picking it out with my gaze. The limited depth of field work favoured by photographers of high end bikes – the kind Portland is famous for making – gives me some comfort that I am not the only poor soul who treasures exquisite bike gear this way and forms emotional bonds with rings of anodized alloys. I was lying before: the bike-love we see in Portland is about far more than just being cool. Bike obsession can happen anywhere.

We trust our lives to these things. We marvel at their efficiency – Steve Jobs almost called his Apple brand 'Bicycle' when he read bikes take us further per joule than even a condor can travel. Of course bikes should be worshiped among tools of locomotion, just as Stradivarius violins are worshiped among musical instruments, or diamonds are worshiped among precious stones. Our shame as a civilization is that the networks of paths we have been providing for these miraculous tools make us look like jewellers mounting diamonds on plastic, or violinists tossing their instruments in with their raincoats. Our shame as architects and urban designers is that we have sat back and allowed by-the-book engineers to design infrastructure for bikes with even less inspiration and care than they would apply when designing a road. It's time someone intervened.

Cycling infrastructure is being upgraded thanks to a confluence of current concerns, which in and of themselves have little to do with the pure pleasures of cycling. The usual arguments for funding new bike paths or reallocating road space for bike use are that cycling keeps people from being inactive, keeps carbon out of the atmosphere and keeps some cars off of roads. It would hardly be so politically palatable to argue that public funds, or public space, should go to indulge the whims of middle-aged men fooling themselves in tight clothes – a stereotype applied to cyclists in many countries.

The danger of focusing on arguments that will win support from all quarters is that bicycling infrastructure is later appraised as though it were a health resource, environmental measure or a pressure valve for traffic congestion, rather than a resource for those who like cycling. What is the harm? Well, if the key performance indicators of a bike path's success trace back to hegemonic concerns rather than the pleasures of self-powered mobility, then whatever infrastructure results from the process could ultimately bring cyclists no joy. We will continue to see chicanes around street bins and phone booths, staccato start-stopping and garish blue painted lanes that make cycling look like the transit equivalent of mini-tennis. In most cities to date the aim has been to make cyclists just safe and happy enough that they don't relapse, rejoin the jam, become unhealthy and pollute the air with emissions.

Let it never be said of architects though that their profession aims to provide enough and no more. Architects are not trained to meet needs, like engineers. They are taught to celebrate aspirations and treat the whole built environment as a platform for art. The architectural imagina-

<u>top</u>
Still from the documen-
tary film *My Playground* by
Kaspar Astrup Schröder
Courtesy of Kaspar Astrup
Schröder

<u>bottom</u>
Kronan underwear bike ad
Courtesy of Kronan Bikes

tion sees Copenhagen trying to raise the bike modal share from one third to one half of all trips and asks what is stopping that city from achieving 100 per cent. Why set targets, or benchmark against rival cities, when the spectre exists for a cycling utopia?

Thinking this way shifts our focus from what environmentalists, health departments or transit planners might want in lieu of support to what motivates those who actually enjoy commuting by bike. This kind of thinking spares us from fallacies like 'Cyclists don't smoke', or 'Cyclists want to save money' or 'Cyclists vote green'. Particular cyclists who don't match these assumptions might be a disappointment to benefactors from health, welfare or environmentalist agencies if any of those thought cyclists were somehow working for them. Transit planners would be especially misguided if they thought cyclists shared their concern with congestion; cyclists adore passing cars caught in jams.

The question of concern to architects is what do cyclists themselves want from roads and cycle path networks?

## How to Read
## Cyclists' Minds

When it comes to understanding cyclists' concerns I would argue surveys are methodologically fraught. How are study group populations selected? How is the manipulation of data prevented? How is it guaranteed that respondents don't lie, saying they're deterred by danger, for instance, because that is easier than admitting they're lazy?

There is also the problem of what authors of surveys call the observer-expectancy effect. Consider a cyclist who has always taken the shortest route between points A and B, irrespective of traffic volume or the avail-ability of bike paths. While this cyclist is clearly unconcerned about the existence of bike paths and is happy to ride among cars, he or she would also be aware that bike paths are political dynamite. Might an answer they give to a researcher sway future planning? Of course their answer has that potential. So where among friends they would have no opinion, an opinion will be captured when they are surveyed. Hot potatoes like hel-met laws, bicycle licences, road tax and even debates about whether or not to wear Lycra all receive much more attention in the press than they do in private conversation.

But even if findings regarding cyclists' concerns could be relied on, architects and urban designers would find these about as interesting as a client's requests for non-slip tiles in their bathroom. Paranoid fears get taken on board, but they are not what inspire great cities or buildings. Architects want to know about their clients most lofty aspirations, some-thing studies to date have not even touched on.

One way of ascertaining what cyclists might want from transit infra-structure without cyclists even knowing they are being observed is to look at how the bicycling industry advertises to its clients. We are not con-cerned if advertising creates or reflects consumer desire. We are simply interested in knowing what cyclists' desires are. And ad tropes give us some marvellous insights.

A moment spent at the newsstand reveals that most of the cycling industry's revenue comes from road racing and mountain biking. Of the remaining specializations that are large enough to warrant magazine titles, the nascent market for upright town bikes is also worthy of study, since this market grows in the wake of bike lane investment. What do ads for upright bikes tell us about what their riders' aspire to get out of cycling?

## Meeting the Aspirations
## of the Cycling World's Chic

The prevalence of straight-backed, well-dressed, beautiful models in advertisements for sit-up-and-beg bikes tells us their buyers are concerned about looking attractive. Bicycle brands like Pashley, Velorbis, Gazelle, Skeppshult, Umberto Dei, Abici, Retrovelo and Batavus, as well as accessory makers like Basil and Brooks Saddles, have all used fashion photography and beautiful models to sell cycling equipment almost as though it were lingerie. Kronan, the Swedish makers of the utility bikes that were used by that nation's soldiers in the Second World War, took the obvious next step of launching their own range of underwear. Thin blonde models raised on diets of muesli and saunas are photographed around Stockholm, supposedly out for a ride in nothing but their sparkling white panties and boxer shorts.

The fully upright riding position is promoted as more comfortable and better for seeing and being seen; but its greater, undeclared advantage is that it doesn't make cyclists look like hunched over apes, but rather fully evolved human beings. Cyclists in posters advertising sit-up-and-beg bikes exaggeratedly thrust their chests out and their shoulders back – a pose observers of body language note we subconsciously adopt when we see someone approaching whom we find attractive. When riding behind ladies in the Netherlands who I have thought were attractive, I have witnessed more than a few glancing at their own reflections in shop fronts. With each glance they push their shoulders back just that little bit more.

Asking why heavy *omafietsen* (or grandma style bikes) are a perennial favourite among female buyers is like asking why so many ladies also like shoes with high heels. There are faster, more practical bikes, just as there are faster shoes. The same is true for gentlemen riders who choose a vintage black roadster to go with their suits.

If we were to use one of the classical labels Greek mythology provides for understanding seemingly irrational human compulsions to explain what motivates aficionados of upright bikes, it would be Eros, a concept Freud related back to Plato's ruminations on *Beauty Itself* in *The Symposium*. The upright bike is a means of commuting, but also of making the scene. Given the choice of two parallel routes, an express lane behind buildings or a pedestrianized mall with bars and cafés, riders of upright bikes would be more inclined to ride down the mall. They wouldn't mind having to slow down for pedestrians, relishing close proximity to potential admirers.

Designing shared zones for cyclists, pedestrians and even some cars if they can be calmed/sedated could benefit from some of the techniques of neighbourhood street design that were pioneered by Dutch traffic engineer Hans Monderman. He believed in putting play equipment and out-door dining tables in the field of view of car drivers as visual cues to make drivers feel they were trespassing in someone's rear yard and to therefore proceed at walking pace. Monderman's is a line of thinking that began with Jane Jacobs' *The Death and Life of Great American Cities*, which notes how groups of children, when they get together in sufficient num-bers, can safely play ball games on local streets despite those streets being open to vehicular traffic. By simply occupying local streets people can tame traffic to the point where we no longer call what results 'chaos'. We call it vitality. Though Jacobs is remembered most for arguing that in-dustrial, commercial and residential activities can all coexist in the same zones, she also brought her idea of a messy vitality to the micro scale of the street, saying it is better to bring fast and slow vehicles together in a way that ensures drivers and cyclists remain vigilant in their duty not to hit children – who will always cross roads without looking – than it is to breed a sense of entitlement among drivers to speed along designated car lanes that children could amble into.

This is a mind-set that can be used to tame bikes as well. Shared zones can use visual cues to remind cyclists where they can and can't ride at full speed. Our lady and gentlemen cyclists on upright bikes may wish to ride between places for seating, but will know from visual cues that they need to ride slowly. Unencumbered swathes through shared zones will naturally funnel the kinds of riders in question next.

### Meeting the Aspirations of
### the Cycling World's Speedy

If advertising tells us riders of upright bikes are the beautiful fashionistas of cycling, it tells us those who shave their legs and wear Lycra are the cycling world's narcissists. As someone who has come from a road racing background, I feel licensed to make such a claim. There are numerous magazines vying for our custom, all with articles about keeping training diaries, adopting that perfect riding position and excises targeting muscle groups unheard of to most. We are a breed of rider who will spend hours reviewing data collected from heart rate monitors, consult sports physi-cians and massage therapists and who can talk about our red blood cells using medical jargon. On the one hand, our aim is to make that state of being 'in form' coincide with particular races we are aiming to win. On the other the obsession with biofeedback, from whatever source, is an end in itself, an end that, like leg shaving or wearing Lycra nicks with no under-pants, has a lot to do with self love.

For the road racing enthusiast, commuting is often viewed as part of a training regime, if not an event in itself. We can, after all, get from door to door quicker than drivers can in the city. Why shouldn't we gloat! We also account for a good deal of the journeys by bike that cities quote in their pre-cycle-path base rates. Sadly, because our intrepidness marks us as highly unusual, new bike plans don't aim at swelling our ranks. Planners know they stand to increase trip-by-bike rates far more if they target that great bulk of households with bikes lying idle in their garages. Around the world, each generation spends billions of dollars on bikes that lay idle. When surveyed and asked why they don't ride, the owners of all this equipment (a form of infrastructure that's going to waste) say they are too frightened of vehicular traffic.

I would contend that no harm can be done to bicycle transit by encouraging competitive road racing, or recreational 'Lycra cycling', among people just wanting to look and feel like pro-racing cyclists. It seems more than a coincidence that bicycle infrastructure in America came in the wake of Lance Armstrong, who raised that country's awareness of road racing. Faux teams in matching jerseys were soon making cycling a part of the national consciousness. Sure, the emphasis was on Lycra cycling. But surely, in a nation where the mere sight of an adult riding a bicycle had been viewed as an oddity, many would not even make a distinction between transit cycling with panniers or cycling in imitation of, or training for, bicycle racing.

But then a few vehicular cyclists in Lycra speak against segregated bike paths – supposedly on behalf of all cyclists – and defenders of slow neighbourhood cycling come out on the defensive, overstating the obvious truth that bicycle transit is mostly pursued by people who have no interest in bikes as sporting equipment. Bicycling lobby groups have been divided between those wanting to ride on the road and those who see roadies as the bane of their quest to build separate bike paths.

In sprawling cities though, there is a connection. For someone whose only experience of cycling has been on bikes with cranky gears and slow-rolling cheap tires, a turn on a race worthy bike with padded nicks and cycling shoes clipped into pedals can come as a revelation. With no cycling fitness at all they find they can actually ride from one side of town to the other, something they might have managed on a slow bike in a dense city in Europe, but could never have dreamed they could achieve in a city like Boston, for instance.

It can be a lonely lot for us roadies, not even having bicycle infrastructure planners advocating on our behalf. Many road riders have no choice but to ride fast: home could be two hours from work if they went any slower. And while most of us own bikes worth 2,000 to 3,000 euros at least, for many roadies their bike is their only indulgence, used on the weekend for recreational racing and all through the week for commuting. For some roadies, cycling long distances to work is a matter of making ends meet, saving on fuel, train fares or bus fares. Their competitiveness and fancy equipment is often just a brave face put on unenviable circumstances.

So when new bike lanes start spouting like churches in the affluent residential districts that long-term cyclists have always passed through on their commutes and they are told this resource isn't for speed freaks in Lycra, road cyclists can be forgiven for feeling betrayed. I realize I am speaking for the slimmest minority, reduced further to those who are easily slighted. Still, they are the ones who cycled all through the bad years. Car commuters who dislike new bike lanes have opportunities to vent to tabloid newspapers and shock-jocks. Long-term cyclists have no voice, save perhaps Eben Weiss, the blogger behind BikeSnobNYC. Weiss laughs off the middle class's latest hypocrisies the way roadies have

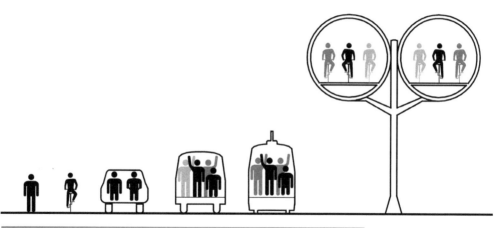

## Velo-City

If architects were engaged to make roadies happy, and given an infinite budget to do so, we might see more proposals like Chris Hardwicke's for Toronto in Canada, which he calls Velo-City. Pairs of glazed tubes – one side heading towards and the other side heading away from the city – would provide cyclists a dream run there and back. Not only do the tubes protect cyclists from the elements, but if many cyclists are using the route at the same time, they will generate their own back draft, helping everyone inside go even faster, compounding their back draft, and so on.

A company called Bicycle Transit Systems (BTS) earlier proposed the same concept, calling it Transglide 2000™. The difference between the two schemes is the images communicating the BTS concept suggested something with as much architectural character as farming equipment. Hardwicke's graphics indicated tempered glass panes and a ribbed struc-tural exoskeleton, recalling Norman Foster's Saint Mary's Axe, whereas the Transglide 2000™ would need to be screened from view using trees. It is better to build for bikes in ways that resonate with trends at the vanguard of public architecture.

Images courtesy of Chris Hardwicke

always laughed off the innumerable ways they have been squeezed out. They can afford to laugh though, because they have spent lives harvesting a resource beyond the reach of anyone but those with the courage to take it. They have free, fast mobility, even in sprawling cities.

While the work of accommodating road cyclists will largely remain the purview of traffic engineers working for departments of transit (who in many cities do a great job), there is a role for architects in making the lives of fast cyclists easier. The most obvious involves the provision of end-of-trip bike parking facilities. Road bikes are expensive and ultra lightweight. If permitted, most roadies would be happiest taking their bikes on their shoulder everywhere that they went: into shops, lifts and even toilets. Short of this, they require secure bike parking facilities, not necessarily out of the elements, but certainly where thieves can't remove pedals that can be worth more than someone else's whole bike.

### Meeting the Aspirations of the Cycling World's Loonies

We have called on Eros and Narcissus, which leaves Thanatos, the figure from Greek mythology now associated with the death drive, who according to Freud compels people to engage in high-risk behaviour. Road cyclists may seem fairly daring when they descend switch-back roads in stage races. Messenger cyclists can appear even crazier, whizzing between cars on their fixies or at worst treating non-consenting cities as courses for 'alley-cat' races. However, mountain bike riders take the award for the most extreme thrill seekers in cycling. Video clips of Red Bull-sponsored downhill mountain bike events posted on YouTube receive millions of views, many times more than other risky kinds of bicycle riding.

Advertisements in mountain bike magazines betray an obsession among this discipline's exponents with peril, particularly during descents. Over and over, photos of riders captured mid air, facing downward, are used to sell everything from the shock absorbers that will catch riders' landings, to the clothes they are wearing, to the drive trains transferring power from their legs to their rear wheels. In the case of that last example it would not be remarked upon that drive trains are largely inactive during descents. They certainly aren't used while bikes are mid air. The advertisers' aim though is not so much to explain the equipment, but to show how close that equipment can bring its owner to the precipice between life and death.

Some might contend that downhill mountain biking has as much to do with bicycle transit as base-jumping has to do with being a pedestrian if a base jumper happens to be wearing walking shoes as they fall. And it is true that compared to someone on a bike fitted with mud guards, lights and pannier bags, the guy in the beetle suit pretending he's sponsored by Red Bull as he floats off of curbs in suburbia is an unlikely contender for the term 'bike commuter'. But if he is making a trip he might otherwise have taken by car, would he not be commuting? And if he has managed to transform a trip to the shops or a friend's house into something exciting, should he not, in some ways, be envied?

In any city with an untamed nature reserve bounded by urban districts, secret sects of off-road commuters cross that land, using trails between trees, many not even known to regular hikers. The World Trail Alliance has increasingly been working with local authorities to develop trails with low environmental impacts that are separate from recreational walking trails. While they are built primarily as recreational amenities, there is no reason why they cannot be viewed as transit infrastructure, if only for a few people who enjoy communing with nature this way.

## Hyperreality

Whether they are riding a retro bike and wearing tweed, dressed up like a bike courier and toting a messenger bag, wearing a pro-cycling team kit, down-hilling on level terrain, or imagining that they are in the Netherlands when in fact they are in Chicago, many cyclists do like to fantasize. In this regard they're exactly like drivers, for whom any city street can be a mountain pass if they are driving an SUV, or any green light the start to a race if they are driving a sports car. Few architects are so dry in their approach that they would not willingly work with users' dreams, taking dreams as the raw material for evocative design work.

Jean Baudrillard's concept of hyperreality provides a useful scaffold upon which such thinking can hang. As Baudrillard sees it, the physical world from which our ancestors reaped crops, or walked in the rain, has been so thoroughly overlain with media images and associated fantasies that the sensorial world of our ancestors is barely perceived. Ontologically, it is the hyperreal world that we inhabit. To be sure, cyclists' bodies are quite often accosted by nature, their physical legs subjected to real aches and their bodies skirt very real dangers that could have drastic repercussions. Despite all of these, though, cycling puts the rider as much in the hyperreal world of media imagery as the empirical world of discomfort and risk.

Imagine the fate of a bicycle by Binachi, cross-branded with the fashion label Armani, that for a spring-season hung in the ION shopping centre in Singapore. Who knows where that bike might be now? It is likely hanging in a small government flat, soothing the pangs of a civil servant who would rather be in Milan than South East Asia.

If only we could follow bikes by Fendi, Gucci, Chanel – almost every fashion house, these days, has its name on a bike – from their starchitect-designed stores in New York or Tokyo to their final resting places on display in living rooms or gathering dust in garages. Given the hand grips and panniers on bikes such as these are worth far more than the steel framed clunkers beneath them, it is hard to imagine any of these bikes getting very much use. But let us not assume all such bikes are of no use at all. They emblemize a cultural turn towards anything healthy, natural and green; a turn away from anything that leaves a large carbon footprint. They stand for the fashionableness and luxuriousness of slowing down.

They also remind architects and urban designers of a different kind of flâneur waiting in the wings, ready to inhabit retail districts and buildings on bikes. The bicycle is providing them with a new way to experience and

1
One Danish study has indicated that the health benefits of cycling to work, and for sport, over a 30-year period, means long-term sports cyclists reduce their risk of death by any cause – *including* accidents – by 40 per cent. See: Lars Bo Andersen, Hans Ole Hein, Peter Schnohr and Marianne Schroll, 'All-Cause Mortality Associated With Physical Activity During Leisure Time, Work, Sports, and Cycling to Work', *Archives of Internal Medicine* (2000) vol. 160, 1621-1628.

admire cities. We already see them inhabiting shopping streets in Milan on a Saturday – in fact, every Italian town on a Saturday. They remind us to stop thinking of retail customers – 'the public' – as always arriving on foot. As the bike modal share rises, more people will be window-shopping while riding their bikes. The architectural imagination, which has no counterpart in the world of traffic engineering or transit planning, is hardwired to embrace changes like these and to please the fashionista on wheels.

And if mountain bike riders were viewed as the end-users of bike infrastructure designed by architects? In that case, the architectural imagination would generate bike transit strategies with scope for excitement. Gullies and ridgelines that have not been developed would be mapped and worked into unpaved transit networks. Parks might include unsealed mountain bike tracks running parallel to those built for more conservative cyclists. Cycling networks would be dotted with BMX courses. The risk to life posed would be no greater than the risk mountain bike and BMX riders seek on their weekends regardless; and pales compared to the risks associated with inactivity.[1]

These recommendations are in the spirit of something architect Bjarke Ingels calls hedonistic sustainability. Propose a diving tower over the harbour in Copenhagen and then watch as people work to clean up the water. Entwine a ramped access balcony throughout an apartment building and watch people choose cycling over driving, because cycling just became fun. Tell the tax payers of Copenhagen they will be able to ski on the roof of a green waste facility and they will be less inclined to complain about the enormous scale of this kind of building, which all cities need to reduce their emissions from waste decomposing.

Fun is an incentive, as can be the invitation to engage in high risk activities. BIG's Mountain Dwellings in Copenhagen's new town of Ørestad are a key setting in Kaspar Astrup Schröder's documentary film about parkour, *My Playground*. The film features interviews with the architect, who plainly delights in seeing his buildings used in these ways.

If parkour has a bicycling counterpart, it is street trials riding. Danny MacAskill, the superstar of that sport, has been featured in dozens of films, riding in impossible ways across rooftops, on handrails and on vertical wall planes. The advertisement he filmed for Volkswagen is his most notable, for the way it uses sculptural buildings in Lisbon as settings for this kind of guerrilla engagement with architecture, in ways that seem intrinsic to architecture when watching MacAskill perform.

Architects and urban designers have never been in the business of making cities just exciting enough that people don't move back to the country. Architecture is building raised to the level of an art form. According to the Vitruvian definition, which still holds in most cases, architecture provides not only firmness and commodity, but some element of delight. We could expect the telltale fingerprint of architects' involvement in cycling infrastructure planning to be liberal servings of smiles.

# Cycle

# Because

# It's

# GREEN

# Chicago

Suppose you wanted to know how cycling would fare with no hindrance or help from roads or transit authorities, purely in response to forces beyond governmental control. You are more interested in ways attitudes about health and pollution, or rising oil prices, or frustrations with traffic contribute to the bike share than whatever impact freshly painted green or blue lanes have on peoples' behaviour. So you come up with the brilliant idea of making a computer model of the most remarkably ordinary city you can imagine, with a view to using this model as your virtual lab.

You might start with a uniform grid, throw in a balanced representation of all the world's cultures and then blanket your model city with a simplistic traffic engineering approach, one that assigns anything that has wheels to the centre of the road and anything without wheels to the edges. To minimize variables you could extend land titles right the way to your notional

river (even hypothetical cities have to have rivers) to prevent opportunistic cyclists from circumventing the grid by riding alongside the riverbanks. Lest your itchy hand later tempt you to intervene with Copenhagen-style bike paths, you could enter a rule that every on-street parking space is to remain sacrosanct, not to be whittled away at with trees, widened sidewalks, bike paths or any such nonsense. Then eliminate the greatest variable influencing the uptake of citizen-cycling by making this Sim-City of yours pancake flat and viola: *The City Itself*, a kind of Platonic Idea in your computer, is ready for testing. Or you could save all that bother and just follow the fortunes of cycling in the Big Onion, Chicago.

There is an architect in Chicago named Brent Norseman who has projects including infill apartment blocks with mansard zinc roofs and a café without WiFi so that patrons are forced to stand at the bar and converse. Resisting American norms in favour of ones from Europe is in some sense Norseman's critical stance. Downstairs from his office is *The Copenhagen Cyclery*, the shop front of another kind of import venture of Norseman's: bringing classic Danish-style cruisers and cargo bikes into the USA. With the imagined European city as his guiding force, Norseman has managed to locate his home, office, shop and even the bulk of his architectural oeuvre in the one neighbourhood, Wicker Park.

The artery of traffic and commerce cutting a diagonal swathe across Wicker Park's street grid is Milwaukee Avenue. Given the increasing volumes of bicycling traffic using this route, bicycling advocates would naturally like to see it reengineered with protected 'Copenhagen-style' bike lanes on either side. So far Chicago's mayor, Rahm Emanuel, has managed to build one such lane in the city, along a half mile stretch of Kinzie Street. Kinzie Street, though, had low volumes of traffic relative to its width: four lanes for driving and two more for parking. Space for cycling could be taken from surplice driving lane space.

The only option on Milwaukee Avenue, since it only has two lanes for traffic, would involve sacrificing lanes used for on-street car parking. Unfortunately, these aren't the city's to take. Chicago's previous mayor, Richard Daley, sold the right to collect parking fees from the city's 36,000 on-street car parking

spaces for 75 years to a Morgan Stanley conglomerate for a one-off lump sum of 1.2 billion dollars. Norseman's hopes for more street trees, alfresco seating and Copenhagen-style bike lanes along Milwaukee Avenue seemed less likely than ever to come to fruition when Daley sold the city's inheritance, metaphorically speaking, to balance the books.

When Norseman loads his kids into his Danish-brand cargo bike and heads to the lake, he has no choice but to take the main roads. There is no bicycle trail alongside the Chicago River, because many private land boundaries have always extended all of the way to its banks. The river's edge never had a chance to evolve into an agreed cycle-space route, the way riverbanks have in most other cities.

Chicago is flat just like the Netherlands; only it has been given over completely to cars. Yet incredibly, it is a great place to cycle – and not only because of the flatness. Approaching the centre of town from whatever direction, building heights steadily rise in this city in such a way that were it not for the lake (that takes the imaginary eastern half and dumps it down there with Atlantis) Chicago would be one giant cone. The lake edge, predictably enough, has become a bicycle superhighway each morning and afternoon. Having an entire half of what would otherwise have been an annular town on a hay plane, surgically removed by a lake, has led to a kind of bloodletting of cyclists. They head straight to the face of the wound. Cars don't do that. Cars follow diagonal expressways into the city.

left
European style housing on North Avenue, Chicago, Norseman Architects, 2008
Photo: Brent Norseman

right
Vehicular cycling in the 'door zone' brings the worst out in everyone, Milwaukee Avenue, Chicago
Photo: Brent Norseman

page 141
Bike traffic in the 'door zone', Milwaukee Avenue, Chicago
Photo: Brent Norseman

pages 142 - 143
Cycle space in Chicago
Photo: Steven Fleming

The main difficulty facing cyclists elsewhere in the city, if we look at what this city was made for, is that anything was ever allowed to go faster than horses and carts. But no one living in Chicago these days is old enough to remember a time before cars. All anyone has ever known are unnatural speeds. Neither would many be able to imagine that ever changing, if for instance a shortage of oil meant streets became so choked with cyclists that cars were slowed to their pace.

Such conditions exist though, on neighbourhood shopping and commercial streets all over the Netherlands. Whole families ride down certain main streets with no separate lanes, cars parked to the side and moving cars in their wake, unable to overtake them. Dutch drivers are so accustomed to cyclists that looking before opening a car door is automatic. We know from these Dutch examples that if nearly everyone in Chicago decided to start cycling tomorrow, the remaining drivers would be tamed by the end of next week. (Many, unfortunately, would be on charges and awaiting their hearings for having hit cyclists.) By the end of next month though, there would be fewer injuries from the rounded bodies of cars, once they are all moving at bike speed, than injuries from riders' own pedals and handlebars.

Chicago may be the last city on earth that will ever get separate infrastructure for cyclists, but the first to prove separate routes aren't always needed. Vehicular transport is dying beneath its own weight. In Chicago rising energy costs, enormous congestion, health consciousness, environmental awareness and the rising cost or parking now that all the spaces are privately owned is increasing the bike share, despite every effort from the car-borne to stop change from happening.

# Chapter 7

# Brownfields to Bikefields

### The Dutch and Danish
### Stories Cannot Be Copied

Infrastructure and laws privileging bicycles over cars in the Netherlands were born of unique circumstances in the early 1970s: hundreds of children killed on their bikes every year, mass demonstrations, car-free Sundays and an oil crisis. We can learn from the Dutch, but treating their story as a meta-narrative, as though strategies they employed can be repeated where politics differ, is folly.

There is, however, a pragmatic approach to achieving more cycling in cities where change is coming too slowly; an approach borne of current political circumstances and the post-industrial urban condition. It involves building bike paths where they don't impact voters who drive – on rail easements, parks, waterways – then rezoning whatever brownfields these paths intersect to permit Bicycle-Oriented Developments (BODs). Like Transit-Oriented Developments (TODs), BODs would be high density, with minimal parking. Developer infrastructure contributions from BODs, as each new one is built, would be spent upgrading bike paths with additional lanes, weather protection and every other convenience.

Instead of pitting cycling against driving in a contest for prime city space, the brownfield-to-bikefield model would have cyclists retreat to an alternative cycle space, which they could gradually develop with cycling as the main emphasis. The better quality of life that cycle space, in time, would provide would likely attract current non-cyclists to live and work there as well. In the meantime, it would provide a safe and fair alternative existence to those who want to orient their lives around bicycle transport.

A comprehensive summary of literature pointing to the societal good that comes from more cycling (coupled with walking) recently appeared in *Built Environment*.[1] The authors, John Pucher and Ralph Buehler, offer eight policy recommendations for encouraging these two active modes, of which at least five punish drivers. They call for:

- 'Better infrastructure for walking and cycling' by giving cars fewer lanes and making them stop more;
- 'Traffic calming of residential neighbourhoods' with obstacles to frustrate car drivers;
- 'Urban design oriented to people and not cars', which would entail clustering shops and attractions around spaces drivers can't easily get to;
- 'Traffic regulations and enforcement', for example Dutch laws that often blame drivers for cyclists' mistakes;
- 'Roadway, parking and taxation policies' that make it more expensive to drive than cycle or walk.

All are policies that have been shown to work in the world's leading bike nations, Denmark and the Netherlands – both nations that perform well in indexes comparing nations' happiness, longevity, mobility, sedentariness and carbon emissions. None of that seems to matter, though, to voters in thousands of the world's middle-sized cities, where driving is

1
Ralph Buehler, John Pucher and Mark Seinen, 'Bicycling Renaissance in North America? An Update and Re-Assessment of Cycling Trends and Policies', *Transportation Research A*, vol. 45 (2011) no. 6, 451-475.

2
For example Copenhagen-
ize Consultancy, Gehl
Architects and Hembrow
Cycling Holidays.

largely delivering on its original promise. Most of the world's cities – if we include all the small ones as well – are not hopelessly crippled by gridlock or shortages of places to park. Voters in places where driving is working have no reason – yet – to heed Pucher's and Buehler's advice.

That doesn't stop progressive thinkers in driving cities from looking longingly to the Netherlands and Denmark. Our envy has created fertile conditions for Dutch and Danish-based planning consultancies, inspirational speakers and bicycle study tour operators ready to show lagging cities how their nations' leads can be followed.[2] Telling (or selling) success stories as things that can be repeated requires the identification of starting points – moments in the past – that resemble moments of today. Jan Gehl identifies such a starting point when he tells how cars were a blight on Copenhagen prior to the introduction of protected bike lanes in the mid 1970s. If bike lanes were a key early first step in the right direction for Denmark, it would follow that bike lanes should be a first priority elsewhere as well.

So how is it going, in the efforts to build Copenhagen-style bike lanes? Your answer is likely to depend on which side you take in a heated debate. Given scholarship in the fields of urban design and town planning overwhelmingly support active transport, most of us in the design and planning community would fall on the side of the Park Slope bike lane in Brooklyn, the Burke Street bike path in Sydney and similar interventions in other cities. We are less sympathetic to drivers complaining about bike paths on talk radio and put the concerns of potential cyclists above those of a handful of intrepid cyclists – the former waiting for bike paths, the latter happy to ride fast among cars. Bike lanes that encourage neighbourhood cycling for transport are consistent with the contemporary planning agenda of building cities for people.

The problem with headlines and debates about bike lanes on major streets is that they steal attention from those places where the great bulk of bicycle commuting is just starting to happen. More cyclists use the Manhattan Waterfront Greenway – a remote place by Manhattan standards – than the Copenhagen-style bike lane on Broadway. In Portland, water's edge routes and rail-trails like the Springwater Corridor are teeming with cyclists at rush hour, while streets redesigned to thwart cars in the gentrified southeast part of town often have scarcely more cyclists than unmodified streets.

Minneapolis, America's no. 2 bicycling city, has little in the way of special road markings or protected bike lanes on roads. Since the passing of the Intermodal Surface Transportation Equity Act (ISTEA) in 1991 – which guaranteed ongoing funding for bike paths – former industrial rail routes, disused industrial rail bridges, land around lakes, land along waterways and land where a century ago there were mills on the banks of the Mississippi have been systematically transformed into a network of bike paths. They are built anywhere except those places people might actually need to find bike paths for getting from point A to point B, and in that sense epitomize a recreational bicycling network. They occupy rail bridges (one sold for less than a euro), contaminated and out-of-the-way places and any other place not contested by voters who drive. Except perhaps for a few streets near the university, the streets of Minneapolis would be more to Henry Ford's liking than any fan of Dutch bike paths. The city's relatively high bicycling use, five times the national average, is attributable to great paths in all the wrong places.

Bicycling advocates striving to replay Dutch history downplay the significance of these hand-me-down spaces, calling them 'recreational' as though they cannot be used to get from home to school, to work or to the shops. In making generalizations like these, bicycling advocates overlook committed cyclists who have been organizing their lives around greenways. For a minority – hardy, devoted, often motivated by fitness – networks of train lines and canals define their mental maps of their city. And where 20 years ago we might have dismissed committed transport cyclists as a fringe group in day-glow, today the regular users of rail-to-trail and waterfront routes can increasingly be seen dressed in school clothes or work clothes, often with shopping bags hanging from their bicycle handles. Greenways have been quietly rising in significance, while bike-lane controversies have been stealing the press.

Unless a pedestrian has been hit by a cyclist on a shared greenway, these places will rarely yield a good headline. However, pro-cycling transportation commissioners and planners are also to blame for not casting a light on the growing role of greenways in transportation. They neglect them because greenways are not a part of the Dutch success story that is now being applied in the manner of a meta-narrative onto the present and into the future.

If we look at the Dutch success story we see many details not matched today. We don't have massive public support for new bike paths today, to compare with the Netherlands' *Einde der kindermoord* (stop the murder of children) rallies in the mid 1970s. Hundreds of children are not being killed every year by cars on their bikes, as was happening in the Netherlands in the 1960s and early 1970s. Modal share base rates for non-cycling nations are less than one tenth of the Netherlands' or Denmark's all-time lows in the 1960s. And don't forget that the first mass cycling era (the 1940s) has now passed from living memory, while in the Netherlands and Denmark that era was still fresh in people's minds when they agreed to revive it. Like any narrative devised to serve a current agenda, the Dutch success story ignores certain facts.

Greenways can't be ignored though, when looking at the recent increase in cycling. Compared to Greenways, Copenhagen-style bike lanes (or 'Tokenhagen' style lanes, as they ought to be called, when they are compromised to the point of not working) look more like broken capillaries than arterial routes. Greenways have done more to help cycling – sometimes without their designers even thinking of cycling – than critical mass demonstrations or rider training programmes or hopeless battles to take space from drivers and give it to cyclists in the form of bike lanes. The only thing we might say against them is that greenways do not link major hubs of activity.

top
1970s rallies in the
Netherlands: 'stop
the murder of children'
Courtesy of National
Archives of the Nether-
lands / Spaarnestad Photo

middle
Broadmeadow Bike
Station, proposed
automated bike parking
tower beside regional
train station,
Newcastle, Australia
Photo: Tom Hatton

bottom
Grassroots tour of
waterway loop by bike
advocates, planners
and environmentalists,
Newcastle, Australia
Photo: Robert Milan

## To Bring the Bike Path to Town,
## or the Town to the Bike Path?

3
The City of Minneapolis
Community Planning and
Economic Development
Department, 'Midtown
Greenway Land Use
Development Plan', 23
February 2007. Available
HTTP: http://www.min-
neapolismn.gov/www/
groups/public/@cped/
documents/webcontent/
convert_266361.pdf (ac-
cessed 16 February 2012).

It is commonplace to say infrastructure attracts new development. Freeways serving no need to begin with can be observed to slowly fill to capacity; the history of urban sprawl is one of roads that first went to no- where. Likewise, we consider it normal, and good, when transit systems are built before the new towns they will ultimately serve. Looking back further, people have built towns next to rivers, but have seldom carved rivers to towns. Why should this principle, that infrastructure paves the way for development, not hold true for bike paths as well?

Recent examples show that it does. Land on either side of the Mid- town Greenway in Minneapolis was rezoned in 2007 to accommodate increasing demand for housing, especially by cyclists reorientating their lives around that fast route across town.[3] A story in the New York Times in September 2011, entitled 'Developers Cater to Two-Wheeled Traffic in Portland, Ore.', tells of dense new housing projects without the normal provisions for parking. Portland has also witnessed entertainment venues targeting bicycling patrons cropping up along major bike routes.

In New York a cyclist's mobility is better the nearer they live to the Manhattan Waterfront Greenway, a safe route that can distribute them to the western end of whichever street they need to go to. Until recently, whatever impetus that bike path was providing for the exiting new archi- tecture going on by the West River could easily have been confused with the impetus provided by a particular aerial park, namely the High Line. However, now that BIG's W57 project is going ahead, beside the bike path but a long way north of the High Line, the greenway's own unique impact can be seen clearly. The success of signature projects near the High Line has in some measure been due to the bike path as well.

These are examples of an organic trend that is occurring in cities with the following three preconditions. First, they are cities where democracy defends drivers' rights, meaning that while government agencies might see the benefits of cycling, politicians are unable to support it in ways that would annoy driving constituents. This gives rise to the second precondi- tion: a flourishing of cycling along networks of railroad land or waterways that predate the roadway network. The passing of these networks' indus- trial functions means they can be turned into greenways. Thus we see contiguous and interdependent networks, which were built for moving commodities, slowly being transformed into networks for moving people on bikes. Finally, these are cities with small factions of highly motivated cyclists. Due to personal motivations to do with their health, pleasure or ideology, these select cyclists ride often, although they don't have to.

When census data indicates a 2 per cent bike modal share in a city like this, we cannot take this to mean 100 per cent of people in that city are using bikes for 2 per cent of their trips, or even that 25 per cent are cycling 8 per cent of the time. Though reliable statistics are not available to determine the precise breakdown, we would be nearer the truth imagin- ing 4 per cent of a population using bikes roughly half of the time – some slightly less, some markedly more. No matter how we decipher available

4
A 2011 study out of Lancaster University found 21.1 per cent of people in Britain often can't use bikes because they must transport children and another 18.4 per cent have this issue sometimes – in other words, primary care givers often and secondary carers when it is their turn to look after their grand kids. See: Colin G. Pooley (corresponding author), 'Understanding Walking and Cycling, Summary of Key Findings and Recommendations' (2011), 11. Available HTTP: http://www.apho.org.uk/resource/item.aspx?RID=111535 (accessed 16 February 2012)

data, we're dealing with a committed minority in cities where bicycle transport remains far from mainstream.

The nascent trend towards building bicycling-oriented developments – near Minneapolis's Midtown Greenway and the Manhattan Waterfront Greenway, for instance – is being fuelled by cyclists like these, who are committed to ride and whose risk aversion means they are motivated to live near the safest bike routes in their city. They lead us to ask if there may not be alternative ways of raising cities' overall bike modal shares, when the Dutch/Danish approach is proceeding at glacial pace. Instead of building bike paths aimed at recruiting cyclists from the non-cycling masses in areas that are unfriendly to cycling, an alternative approach might be to help the committed and risk-adverse cyclists use bikes for more of their trips. If the greenways they lived near were upgraded with lights for the night time as well as rain canopies and fast and slow cycling lanes, nothing might deter those choosing bike friendly areas from using their bikes all of the time: not darkness, rain, fear of fast riders, impatience with slow riders or the need to escort children on bikes.[4] Hypothetically speaking, a city's overall bike modal share could be doubled, not by doubling the number of cyclists but by doubling how often that city's existing stock of cyclists are riding.

The Dutch/Danish story calls for safe bicycling access wherever roads go in order to bring bike paths to people and to make cycling mainstream. Tellers of this story forget that cycling, though it went through a period of decline in the 1960s, has always been mainstream in these countries. Elsewhere, though, transportation cycling has become an alternative lifestyle choice. It seeks to eke out a space in the city in the same way that ethnic, gay and bohemian communities look for neighbourhoods where individuals can flourish in the company of like-minded people. The most we can do for current non-cyclists, once we have found the bike friendly parts of our cities, is to make our lives there so enviable that they relocate and take up cycling as well.

## The BOD Funding Cycle

The brownfield-to-bikefield model does not fight political reality by starting out trying to service established urban districts with bike paths. It starts by developing new urban districts near bike paths that already exist and that are already luring in cyclists. By ensuring that funds raised through developer infrastructure contributions are spent on upgrading bike paths (and not siphoned off to pay for roads), the brownfield-to-bikefield model makes bicycling districts even more attractive to cyclists, thus attracting developers to build more housing for the growing bicycling market, thus generating funds for even more upgrades to bike paths, and so on.

The world has not seen bike paths of the quality that could result if BODs and bicycle infrastructure were tied to each other and left to snowball. On routes linking large BODs we could be looking at bike paths with multiple lanes, lights, canopies, no on-grade interface with cars at all, real-time data analysis and surveillance and perhaps even back-drafting. Small BODs scattered over large areas would give rise to more diffused networks of less extravagant bike paths.

It will fall to governments to set in place the planning laws and funding regimes that would make up two thirds of a self-feeding planning and funding regime. Before they would do that, they would need to recognize the BOD as an alternative development paradigm, not catering for whole populations but for the percentage of a city's population that happens to be willing to orient their lives around bicycle transport. Granted, their transportation needs might be augmented using car sharing schemes, mixed-mode journeys and walking. Cycling, though, would be their mainstay.

Choosing any neighbourhood means limiting your access to others, and likewise, choosing a BOD means less frequent visits to friends and family in car dominated parts of one's city. It also means looking for schools, shops and work that you can reach via a network of bike paths. The BOD, though, is not being held up as a blanket solution. It belongs to an alternative mapping layer that we can trace across cities and in that way accommodate the needs of a hitherto overlooked group: people who are committed to cycling. Recognizing their existence and their desire to have land developed in a way that suits their lifestyle choice would lead to new zoning laws specific to BODs.

While it would be impossible to anticipate the precise mix of guiding principles that each of the world's local governments might devise for their BODs, it is easy to generalize. BODs will surely have: deterrents to car use; higher density relative to better access to bike paths (not roads or transit); mixed use to encourage light industrial, commercial and public facilities (especially schools); and hyper bike-friendly buildings. Governments' other obligation to the long-term success of BODs will be to ensure that developer infrastructure contributions, plus a fair proportion of residents' city or land taxes, are directed towards bike infrastructure. They will need to put laws in place similar to the 1991 Intermodal Surface Transportation Equity Act (ISTEA) in Minneapolis that provide a fair and reliable funding stream for ongoing upgrades and expansions to each city's bicycling network.

However, before creating new zoning rules or putting in place laws that ensure revenue is spent on bike paths and greenways, governments need to be confident that BODs will be used.

## If BODs are Built,
## Will People Come?

What indications are there that people will choose lives of bicycle dependence in high-density developments with limited access to cars or public transport? Anyone in the habit of leaving home in their car or walking from their home towards buses or trains might find it hard to imagine anyone prioritizing access to a bike path over access to parking or transit.

To many living lives of car and/or transit dependence, bicycle dependence is simply unthinkable. Even regular cyclists are cable of reverting to the machine dependence imprinted on them since childhood, when all trips except local ones were by bus, train or their parents' cars. I was a habitual cyclist when I first went to Amsterdam in 1998. Even so, it didn't occur to me to hire a bike. Instead I wasted money, and much of my time, using buses and trains.

Using bicycle transit as a basis for development is so radical that it can only proceed with tentative steps. Thus cities are likely to approach the BOD experiment cautiously at first – much the way individuals experiment with riding to work. Bicycle commuting is something many people don't imagine themselves ever doing, until suddenly they have done it once and are doing it often. Many take it up after witnessing other people who they can relate to – for example other non-sports people – leading the way. Seeing cycling working for somebody else is the empirical catalyst to a process of reasoned deductions concerning health benefits as well as the cost and time savings that inspire people to invest in a modest priced bike and give bicycle transport a try. Then, if they overcome early setbacks – like their first puncture or ride in the rain – converts to bicycle transport might expand the role bikes play in their lives. But it all begins with that first ride.

It would likewise be natural for cities to zone a few trial parcels of land and start out with a small number of BODs. One indicator to help chose areas where these developments have a chance to succeed is if bike paths have increased property prices there and/or if they have been a catalyst for bicycle-orientated development of the kind already happening in Portland and Minneapolis. We can then reason that demand for such property is only likely to increase as a result of: an increasing shortage of affordable housing in many cities throughout the world; rising energy prices; peoples' awareness of their own health and that of the environment; and increasing congestion on roads. But it all begins with that first specially-zoned parcel of land. If it is successful more BODs can follow.

### Urban Renewal If
### Cycling Came First

Though most of the world's cranes seem to have been shipped over to China and the economic climate in Western Europe and North America would seem to preclude any large visionary projects, planning continues on some truly bold urban renewal projects. There is the roughly 56,650-hectare urban park Millennium Reserve, planned for the former industrial land stretching across the south of Chicago. London's 2012 Olympic Games has given that city new wetlands, a technology park, housing and a university, all on former brownfields. The Los Angeles River is due to be transformed from a drain into somewhere to watch birds and ride bikes. The BeltLine in Atlanta will transform 35 km of former industrial rail corridors and factory sites into a green transit loop dotted with affordable housing and parks. These are behemoth projects backed by legions of stakeholders, investors and, most importantly, voters. Each will release a good deal of its city's locked-up cycling potential.

Plans to let bicycles into these projects are like the first modernist house plans that let kitchens into main living areas: they are being made with no appreciation of the magnitude of what is about to be unleashed. Cooking, once let into spaces for entertaining, went from being a chore to a performance, with the living room as its theatre and the kitchen its stage. Planners assume their expensive light-rail systems will be the centre pieces of their urban renewals, forgetting greater amounts of money have already been spent filling garages around the world with bicycles that can't be ridden because of unsafe roads. Letting cycling be a part of all these prime public spaces rather than relegating bikes to roads made for motorized vehicles will unlock a vast amount of infrastructural resources. The 2011 Australian National Cycling Participation Survey found that Australians have 1.6 working bikes in every household. Not including bikes in need of minor repair and conservatively guessing just 400 euros was spent to purchase each working bike, Australia's 7.6 million households are sitting on over 5 billion euros worth of transport equipment that has no purpose-built network to run on. By all means, lay tracks for light rail, just remember that you will have to build the trains too. Meanwhile, bike paths stand to fill up right away.

The colossal urban renewals listed above are plausible because many people can see themselves reflected in them. These range from large players such as developers, environmental agencies and water management authorities to individuals with interests as diverse as bird watching, bass fishing and cycling. I'm sure it could be logically argued, or shown through survey data, that of all the singular activities and agendas these projects appeal to the opportunity afforded to boost bicycle transport would rate as the most agreed upon positive outcome. Even if they don't cycle themselves, most would find some grounds (health, global warming, reduced parking demand, tourism, etcetera) upon which to give cycling a go. So, when identifying strategies for redeveloping underutilized former industrial land, why not prioritize cycling right from the start?

I recently took a large-scale map of my city, Newcastle, Australia and highlighted every rail easement, storm water drain and park that could possibly be taken as the course of a new off-road bicycling route. In another colour I highlighted the underutilized industrial land in the city as well as contaminated sites (for example our former gasworks). Through this exercise I learned that most of the redevelopment sites in this city could be linked by the creeks. Styx Creek and Cottage Creek flow eastward and run into Throsby Creek, along which there is already a bike path. To the west the upper reaches of Styx and Cottage Creeks have tributaries fanning out into the suburbs. A tributary reaching north from Cottage Creek almost reaches a tributary reaching south from Styx Creek. Bike paths following these tributaries would come close to forming a loop – and would do if a short on-road bike path was marked on the quiet street linking these ends.

Such a loop would serendipitously pick up all the bike trails from the suburbs that currently break down as they reach the city. It would pass high schools and most of the sporting venues that kids go to after school for sports practice. Our city's technical college, a shopping mall, farmers markets, the football stadium and some manufacturing sites that still remain viable would all be connected.

The redevelopment sites linked by the loop could not only be used to address the city's own shortage of affordable housing, but also to relieve population pressures on nearby Sydney. Funds raised via developer infrastructure contributions from all of that housing would be sufficient to pay not only for great bike paths, but also recreational amenities and waterway remediation along the full length of the loop.

Conventional wisdom would call for a light-rail system to follow that loop and justify higher densities on the brownfields along it. But this loop is just 7 km long. The entire loop could be travelled in less than a half hour by any Dutch mum on a box bike filled with groceries and children, or by an invalid on a mobility scooter, or even by an Australian who hasn't ridden a bike since childhood. Factor in express lanes and overpasses where those bike paths cross all the roads and you would find a keen cyclist could circle the loop in less than 15 minutes. In a velomobile they might complete it in less than ten!

A vibrant and happening corridor for active transport would accommodate speeds ranging from that of the sports cyclist's to that of a mobility scooter and would ensure others could still use the space like a park. With the techniques of separation designers are used to employing – varying paving materials, stratification by levels, planting, etcetera – it should be possible to design any short stretch according to place-making principles, with conflicting activities such as living, working, shopping, farming, playing and travelling at various speeds using bikes. Daunting as all that may seem, it would not be as difficult as designing quality streets that also need to accommodate cars and trucks. The formulaic approaches of engineers can be discarded in favour of the creative ones that architects use. No two stretches of cycle space need ever be exactly the same.

### Inviting Non-Cyclists to Cycle Space

The process of identifying, conceptualizing, gathering support for and ultimately realizing urban renewal schemes while giving primacy at every stage to the bike rider needn't be to the exclusion of the non-cyclist. I say that as a cyclist who gets as annoyed as any other at pedestrians waddling all over my bike lane, deaf to my bell because of their headphones. But let's maintain some perspective. Pedestrians are only a menace where they outnumber bikes. As the number of cyclists increases – as they inevitably would do in places conceived from the outset to provide a good bike ride – pedestrians learn to walk near the edge and keep control of their children. And from a cyclist's perspective I can tell you that pedestrians, when they're outnumbered and have been properly trained, give me as much of a boost as lines of cars stuck in traffic. They make me feel fast, fearsome and envied. So let's admit that we want non-cyclists around to give us an audience and for their political and economic support for renewal projects that will help cyclists.

The next logical step would be to convert people who are strolling to rolling. Cities including Paris and Barcelona have made thousands of new recruits by introducing bike sharing schemes. The largest bike share in the world ever is about to descend on New York: 10,000 bikes across 600 stations, and that's just stage one of the scheme.

Most cities with bike-shares have included baskets on their fleets of bikes. In the interests of broadening the appeal of bike-focused urban renewals it would be worth considering the addition of fleets of free-to-use bikes that looked more like shopping trolleys, only with seats and pedals somewhere. That way the loop would satisfy the perennial interest in shopping, which far outweighs our culture's interest in cycling, with a novel new way to shop-'til-you-drop (off of your bike-trolley). If it meant garnering support for great bike infrastructure, I wouldn't mind if bicycling districts had parking lots to one side to encourage residents of car-lands to visit and pick up a trolley.

A populist approach to the programming of these bike-focused urban renewal schemes would help quieten rumblings that we – the urban elite – only ride because we are pious. It would seem politically prudent to include skate parks, playgrounds, BMX tracks, bass or trout fishing ponds, rowboat concessions or any activity not automatically seen as the purview of sanctimonious yuppies. The bird habitats, urban farms and fair trade cafés are bound to come anyway.

Inviting car-loving suburbanites to come, shop and be entertained would have little chance of diluting these areas' bicycling flavour. These areas would, after all, belong to extensive systems planned from the out-set to meet broader bike infrastructure demands. They would give people living within their boundaries opportunities to organize their lives around bicycle transport rather than just seeing bikes as feel-good adjuncts to lives otherwise dependent on owning a car. They would give people an opportunity to tackle all of the details of a life in the saddle, like choos-ing suitable clothing to cope with the rain or learning how to fix flats on the roadside, transporting children to their grandparents' for visits and knowing what to do with goods bought at one store when chaining up and entering the next store. They would learn to overcome all the complica-tions part-time cyclists use as excuses to drive.

For their part, architects working in places like these will have to: stop using square lift carriages; look at the ground plane as something that ought to be gently undulating in order to store and release potential energy, so riders can speed up and slow down without braking or standing out of their saddles; start designing paths that respond to ways cycling can be sexy, sporty or suave (all indulgences granted to drivers); start placing bike racks where thieves can't be sure the owner is not observing their suspicious behaviour; look for creative means of providing weather protection to bike routes; design way-finding that does away once and for all with the need for special bike maps; and generally stop seeing cars as a fall-back to justify inadequate provisions for bikes.

We are talking about cities within cities affording hard core believers in bike dependence the opportunity of never leaving – of raising their children to only know cars as those things they see from overpasses. Non-cyclists en-tering systems of bicycle-oriented urban development might feel like visitors to a separatist zone or like tourists walking into the self-proclaimed free dis-trict of Christiania, in Copenhagen. Christiania was established in 1971 when bohemians took over disused military barracks and implemented a policy of banning cars from the site altogether; a policy that has held fast until today.[5] What is most surprising about this story is that within a few years of Chris-tiania's establishment as a car-free, bicycling zone, people throughout the rest of Copenhagen were mounting the large-scale pro-cycling rallies that led to the construction of that city's bicycling infrastructure.

5
Critics object that Christiania is no longer populated by so many idealists. Today a signifi-cant number of residents own cars that they leave parked just outside Chris-tiania's boundaries.

# Cycle

# Because

# It's

# THEATRICAL

# Paris

Paris is a hostile city for cycling. Planning trips using the bike map is a complete waste of time, with something like a third of the protected bike lanes illegally used for car parking at any time and shared lanes dominated by pushy drivers of busses and taxis. The way cyclists are made to circle monuments while merging with motorized traffic is so fraught with danger it must contravene some UN convention. Most callus of all is a theory behind much of the city's bike planning: that thousands of cyclists released on the streets will tame the mopeds and cars and thus make everyone safer. Yes, it's unnerving knowing you are being used as a human shield, that the real price of riding those ridiculously cheap city bikes includes donating your body for traffic calming.

But Paris has always been callus, not only to cyclists, and cyclists would not be the first ones who needed safe havens they could retreat to. The covered shopping arcades that were invented by the French after their revolution were an escape for pedestrians from the hostility of streets when streets gave reign to horses and carts. Pedestrians lined their covered arcades with shops and as many mirrors as King Louis XIV had installed in his palace in Versailles, and there began their lives of *flâneuring*, shopping, eating in restaurants and generally being bourgeois.

Not all French experiments in architectural escapology have been as successful as the arcades. The mid-twentieth-century idea of raised walkways between buildings, making a new ground plane away from the traffic, has been a disaster at La Défense. All those footbridges are windblown and freezing, without the shops or cafés that Parisians enjoy on the street.

They make a disorientating maze with parts closed off after hours and so many stairs where levels don't mesh that cyclists and the disabled are better off on the ring road below.

At least we can say of La Défense that it is inventive. But then the French are inventive – and I'm not just talking about the derailleur – one of their great contributions to cycling. Philosopher Jacques Derrida invented deconstruction, a form of semiotic analysis of text showing how apparent meanings can be inverted. Later architect Bernard Tschumi invented ways of applying deconstructivism to architecture, in the Parc de la Villette. That park's industrial looking wheels that don't turn, its follies with forms that don't follow their functions and other absurdities heralded a paradigm shift in architectural thinking. Sometimes it is more sensible not to make sense with design.

Reading this park in a structuralist way would have us interpreting it as a nice place to walk or kick a football around. But Derrida's philosophy invites illegitimate readings that run against the grain of what might seem obvious. Thus, while Tschumi hasn't catered terribly well for bike commuters – making them cross the canal via steep stairs, for example –

he ought to be pleased local cyclists don't see a park either to stroll in or play football. Many cyclists would interpret Tschumi's park as an expressway between the various neighbourhoods that it abuts.

Contrasting the desperation of cycling elsewhere in Paris, the Parc de la Villette serves cycling as a pleasurable end in itself. Here cycling is not just a last ditch means to reduce time spent commuting. There are children and families on bikes here as well as elderly cyclists and bike riders in lycra. The park gives them the same kind of respite from hostile streets that covered arcades gave pedestrian shoppers in the late eighteenth century.

If we think of the Parc de la Villette as a kind of arcade for high-speed *flâneurs*, we can start identifying sites for

interconnecting arcades. The park is cut by Napoleon's Canal Saint-Martin and though they haven't been yet, the banks of that canal could be conceptualized as bicycling highways extending south to the Seine. The Seine likewise has banks with undeveloped cycling potential. Just to the south of the Parc de la Villette, Canal Saint-Martin intersects Paris's La Petite Ceinture (Little belt railway), an extensive tram corridor that has been abandoned since the 1930s. This grown-over old easement almost makes a complete ring around Paris and features enough high-lines and tunnels that it could become one of the most theatrical urban greenways yet to be built.

That greenways be theatrical seems vital in Paris. Tables outside restaurants in this city all face the street, so couples can sit and watch passers-by rather than facing each other. Tables are also packed so tightly together that each restaurant looks like a packed theatre looking upon the street as though it was a stage. In that case the latest show to hit town is bicycle transport.

Despite all their shortcomings, bike lanes with Velib stations every 300 m have made cycling a significant part of Parisian street life. Thousands of vintage Peugeot racers and *mixte* (unisex) bikes have been reconditioned and added to the city's privately owned fleet that also includes vintage roadsters, French *porteur* bikes, designer bikes, messenger bikes, Dutch cargo bikes and any other bike type that garners attention. As for clothes, one simply doesn't wear stretch pants to cycle in Paris. One dresses to be admired, with a scarf perhaps and a messenger bag matching the colour of one's shoes and Brooks saddle. Compared to the Danes, say, or the Northern Italians, who look elegant on their bikes, Parisians have a way of looking assembled. They dress for their ride knowing the street will be their catwalk.

If ever Paris gets greenways – bicycling arteries, not mere capillaries – those greenways likewise have to double as stages. They need to be laced with restaurants and bars and be more than just routes to get from here to there. And like the rest of Paris, those greenways should be lined with mirrors.

# Chapter 8

# Some Nice

# Looking

# Detours

## The Architecture
## of Cycle Space

A new age of cycling is upon us, complete with new types of bikes and cycling technology. This means we can't really compare cycling now to what it was in the 1940s or how it developed in Dutch urban centres. Cycling today is potentially fast and long reaching, yet at the same time accommodating of children, people with loads and those with disabilities. With some electric assistance, anyone from age 8 to 80 can tackle a hill or cross a whole city.

So in a time when cycling can be enjoyed by anyone, urban designers need to address how it can be enjoyable to everyone. Similar to the 1960s realization that the pedestrian's experience of cities was being neglected, today we realize the cyclist's experience needs a lot more attention.

Going back a bit further, to the interwar period, it is notable that theorists of that time who were excited about the potential of cars hadn't actually begun to aestheticize the driver's experience. That step would come a few decades later with books like *Learning From Las Vegas*. In the interwar period though, freeways and elevated point blocks were embraced, not because anyone was imagining driving itself being beautiful but because architects envisioned lots of beautiful green space resulting from freeways. Le Corbusier wasn't interested in the view through the windscreen but in the views of rolling green landscapes he imagined cities could provide if they were planned around freeways.

This is one reason why the next wave of theorists, the urban designers, spoke of 'streetscapes' and 'townscapes'. They were looking for alternatives to offer once it was realized cities could never really edify our eyes with rolling green landscapes. If we look at Gordon Cullen in particular, the inference is that someone designing a 'townscape' – the kind of 'scape' that most concerned Cullen – is acting in the manner of one designing a traditional English estate, only instead of presenting the walking viewer with an unfolding series of landscape images (lawns, follies) they are presenting the viewer with an ever unfolding series of townscapes. What is a townscape? It is like landscape, only it is not out on the land: it is in town. Though I'm sure Cullen would object to my saying so, the concept of townscape revolves around pretty pictures with towns as their subjects.

Urban streets in Cullen's thinking are like the cliff faces lining the River Wye, which William Gilpin described as though they were being presented as pictures for his own visual consumption. That was the birth of the picturesque, a way of seeing nature, art and architecture that gives primacy to a viewer, specifically a viewer who moves. Cullen's is a picturesque approach to urban design, centred on the visual experience of the pedestrian, apprehending streets, piazzas and gateways. I am proposing Cullen's thinking about townscapes evolve to take account of a new point of view, that of the cyclist.

The cyclist's point of view speeds up as it goes downhill, decelerates as it rises, leans as it turns and when at speed sees fine-grain detail as merely a blur. Pedestrians plod along at roughly the same speed all the time, regardless of gradient. When designing for people who will be viewing the world from a bike we can start with the assumption that riders

top
Cyclists forced to cross
canal using stairs, Parc
de la Villette, Paris
Photo: Steven Fleming

middle
Cyclists preparing
to scramble, Paris
Photo: Steven Fleming

bottom
Cyclist about to receive
a 'right hook' from a
driver who hasn't looked
before turning
Photo: Steven Fleming

will move on a ground plane designed to optimize the cycling experience. Road design guidelines and even guidelines for the design of bicycle infrastructure are not as concerned with optimizing the cycling experience as with merely making bicycling possible in a world that has been overrun completely by cars. Spaces that are purpose-built for the pure joy of cycling, like velodromes and BMX tracks, provide a more joyful lead to thinking about cyclescapes.

These two rare kinds of undulating surfaces, built especially for bicycles, convert potential energy into kinetic energy and vice versa. Consider the banked corners on BMX tracks. These reduce riders' speed so they can change course without losing traction on a loose surface. Once on their new trajectory, the BMX riders' lost kinetic energy that was momentarily stored in the form of potential energy due to their elevation in height is delivered straight back. Let this be the first principle of cyclescaping then: cyclists will have their speeds reduced at destinations and intersections and then increased for transit by the way ground planes are designed to gently undulate. Places to ride slow, such as approaches to buildings and intersections, will ideally be slightly elevated and areas that exist to be traversed will be sunken.

A piazza in cycle space would be shaped like a basin. Freestanding buildings would be located on mounds (doubly useful, as the waterways and flatlands I am proposing we develop for cyclists are often flood-prone). Streets would be U-shaped in section, naturally slowing cyclists as they veer towards the edge and bringing them back to speed as they rejoin bicycling traffic.

We would be looking at a ground plane with no parallel in the history of architecture. Its nearest cousins, aside from velodromes and BMX tracks, would be skate parks, snowboarding half pipes and ski fields, rolling oceans, and skies concealing thermal updrafts from all eyes but those of birds and those trained to fly gliders. But none of those environments have produced architecture. No one has thought about what kinds of built environments (or cyclescapes) would evolve if everyone in the city were dipping into basins and seeing the world as a blur, leaning through corners and thus seeing buildings around them all arching over, and slowing as they ascended onto higher planes where they would once more see things in detail. Never before has a whole built environment been conceived through the eyes of a cycle-born population, using a ground plane sculpted first to meet their needs, not those of pedestrians or users of cars.

By yet another accident though (like the accident that saw cycling benefit from attempts to make reclaimed industrial areas conducive to walking) many architects and urban designers are already conceiving their buildings from points of view that are more like cyclists' than those of ambulatory users of buildings. They design using software that allows them to review their work using fly-through animations. Winning or losing clients, and design competitions, often depends on how schemes appear from those fast moving, arcing view points, sometimes airborne, but as often at eye level or slightly higher, these being the viewpoints that characterize fly-through animations.

The animation produced by BIG in its bid to redesign Slussen (Stockholm) resembles helmet-cam footage. Next we notice how the radii of their ramps, promenades and the buildings belonging to their ensemble seem to have been carved from solids and planes by that fast-flowing viewer. Put simply, their scheme has been designed to look good in a fly-through. Even though their public place, as it is presented, shows more pedestrians than cars or cyclists, the presentation method betrays the designers' own doubts about the pedestrian experience, which could be quite boring. The project would look better and is unintentionally designed to look better when experienced from a point of view most like that of a cyclist's. Looking at how straight walls are vertical and how curved ones are leaning, we can see our own way of moving on bikes echoed in BIG's proposed buildings at Slussen. Much of the fluid, curvilinear, non-planar architecture being produced in this age of computer aided manufacturing and fly-through visualizations would seem entirely fitting in a city conceived as a cyclescape.

The Australian architecture firm Lahz Nimmo has won a competition to build an underpass beneath a typical vehicular cloverleaf in Australia's national capitol, Canberra, with a scheme incorporating similar fluid geometries to those BIG used at Slussen. The outer retaining wall of Lahz Nimmo's slice through the earth (recalling Maya Lin's Vietnam Veterans Memorial) is vertical where it is straight and leaning where it is curved. It mirrors the arcing motion of bicycles beside it. In the tradition of picturesque approaches to urban design, with their emphasis on framing the view for the moving spectator, Lahz Nimmo's underpass is designed to frame views for fast moving cyclists of the National Carillon (1970), a key local landmark by architects Cameron, Chisholm & Nicol.

### Urban Morphology

In addition to their picturesque studies of townscapes and streetscapes, early urban designers popularized the use of figure/ground plans. These served them in numerous ways, first as tools for analysing the traditional European cities that were inspiring them, then to yield memorable images of ideal urban morphologies that designers like Leon Krier hoped others might keep in the back of their minds when designing new towns. Most importantly, drawings like these left no doubt about urban designers' reactionary stance against Le Corbusier.

The most conspicuous feature of Le Corbusier's and his followers' visions were the towers and slab blocks. However, we should not forget these were designed in the service of the landscaped planes in their shadow. The only reason the buildings were so tall, and hoisted higher still on slender columns (piloti), was to leave the landscape below undisturbed. In modernists' imaginations there would be no figure at all in a figure/ground image, just tiny black dots left by the thinnest imaginable columns.

The planes of most interest to urban theorists reacting against Le Corbusier were not grass covered and horizontal, but vertical and made of brick. Ideally permeated with shops and cafés at ground level and elegantly fenestrated from the awning height to the datum height regulating all of their parapets, horizontal wall planes would define some outdoor spaces as streets, others as piazzas and occasionally mark gateways and nodes. The ideal figure/ground plan in the imagination of the postmodern urban theorist resembles a labyrinth, but one that pedestrians will ultimately feel proud to have conquered, courtesy of an arsenal of axes, vistas and landmarks designed to stop them from ever getting too lost.

Why, though, have urban designers agonized about ideal urban patterns? Are they not, with each design choice, merely attempting to overcome deficiencies of the body, in the city, without a bike? Wouldn't all of this visual stimulation and intrigue they are trying to create for the viewer be unnecessary if walking was not so boring and slow in the first place? And would not their obsession with passive surveillance be unnecessary as well if it weren't for the fact that walking makes us slow moving targets of crime, praying that other pedestrians might witness our attackers and intervene? Pray as we might, pedestrians are hopeless at providing surveillance. Their own slowness has them clustering around a few main shopping streets, leaving most city streets desolate except for passing cars.

And what help are drivers?! Inside their machines they *become* their machines, convinced they have no choice but to proceed at, or above, the speed limit, no matter what harm they might cause or what human suffering their speed makes them blind to. This pathology of driving could hardly be said to be true of people on bikes. Cyclists' flesh and blood bodies are on the street, not in a car, and this insinuates cyclists in civic life. This is borne out by the true, if unlikely, story of London's mayor Boris Johnson averting a bashing that he suddenly came upon when riding his bike.[1] It demonstrates the way cyclists are naturally engaged with life on the street and at the same time capable of providing the kind of omniscient passive surveillance we wish for from drivers but can never count on, because drivers are too safely shut off.

Cyclists in the city are reassuring to others and not themselves paranoid. The best news for planners though, is that cyclists are not easily bored. I know I would be just as happy crossing a Corbusian park with towers above as I am riding on lonely plains. Medieval towns have their delights, though I admit acute city blocks and blind corners can slow me down – rush hour cyclists in Amsterdam would make much better time if it weren't for blind corners. Something like the chamfered perimeter blocks of Barcelona's Eixample district would provide a better cycling experience.

In summary, though, I would rather this section be taken as my apology for not suggesting an ideal urban morphology for cycle space. Every combination of site constraint and building type will call for its own urban texture, happily unencumbered by lofty ideals or anxious attempts to make the world less boring or scary for people on foot. Perimeter blocks will still be of worth, but urban districts could perform equally well if made up of freestanding buildings conceived to be viewed in-the-round, or even raised on piloti.

## Building Typology

The brownfield-to-bikefield scenario identified in the previous chapter, which would see development on brownfield sites flanking existing and potential bike routes along rail corridors and waterways, is likely to give rise to more bike friendly buildings like 8-House. Since it would be bicy-

1
See http://news.bbc.
co.uk/2/hi/8340865.stm
(accessed 19 August 2011).

2
Lars Bo Andersen, Hans
Ole Hein, Peter Schnohr
and Marianne Schroll
'All-Cause Mortality
Associated With Physical
Activity During Leisure
Time, Work, Sports, and
Cycling to Work', *Archives
of Internal Medicine* (2000)
vol. 160, 1621-1628.

cling infrastructure driving demand on these sites, we can assume many buyers would be attracted to developments that not only provided bicycle parking, but that promoted a bicycling life.

Many factors point to a rise in demand for buildings that better accommodate bikes. Rising oil and electricity prices will invariably convert more people to cycling, who will surely start looking afresh at high-density housing if it offers shorter bike rides to work, school and shops. These won't only be struggling students, outcasts and eccentrics; stereotypes like those stand to blind planners to an increasing prevalence of well-to-do cyclists, particularly ones in their old age looking for accommodation within bicycling range of varied amenities. We've seen how – even when accounting for accidents – cyclists live longer.[2] They can also keep riding long after failing eyesight or wits has forced their car dependent contemporaries to give up their licences and go back to using buses and taxis. Thus in bicycle-oriented development zones the proportion of cyclists among older age groups could be expected to go up, rather than down.

Of particular interest to speculative developers would be the added wealth enjoyed by most cyclists. The extra car never bought by a medium- to high-income family with one or more keen cycling members will have saved them around 750 euros per month on depreciation, registration, insurances, fuel and repairs. That sum invested each month, with gains of 10 per cent per annum, would grow to 1.7 million euros in one mortgage period of 30 years. From a fringe group, the bicycling demographic is set to become one that developers will target as aggressively as they have targeted empty nesters of the baby boom generation.

What might such buyers be drawn to? First we should acknowledge that certain cyclists would sooner be sent to live in Siberia than a spec-built apartment development and would be most drawn to old inner-city neighbourhoods reflecting the anti-capitalist values that for them cycling grows out of. A remaining portion though, would of course be attracted to developments that made leaving home on a bike as easy as the garage-fronted house has made leaving home in a car. The complete real estate package in the age of the bike in districts planned around bicycle transit will be the apartment with a ride-in bike room with space for bikes owned by the whole household. It will be part of a building with a continuous access ramp, joined seamlessly with bike paths at ground level. That's the ideal: buyers of second-best buildings will have to make do with generous lifts, ramps beside stairs, ground-level secure bike parking areas and eyes on racks positioned where bike thieves might otherwise be tempted to lurk.

### Market Driven or
### Government Mandated?

Peak oil will pinch. A portion of the population, though its size may be undeterminable, will vote with their feet to use bikes, largely to save money but also to beat traffic, keep fit and for the sheer enjoyment of cycling.

Enough motivations, for enough people, exist that we can be confident of at least some market demand for bike-friendly buildings. But could governments legislate for them as well?

Outside of the Netherlands, where building codes have mandated bicycle storage rooms for houses and flats (at least, that was the case until 2003), governments seem far too beholden to voters who drive to ever make blanket rules with more than token impact. The dynamics of the situation are apparent in the way green building certification instruments take no serious account of energy used bringing people to and from buildings. In fact, it can be easier to achieve LEED certification in the USA or 5-Green-Stars in Australia when designing on greenfields beyond the reach of bike paths and public transport than in the city, where contextual constraints limit access to the sun and demand more energy-intensive construction methods. Why don't more thinking observers object? In many cases, it could be due to their own car addiction – addicts have blind spots. A lauded green building with a huge car park is as self-evident to the car addict as an obligatory bottle of wine with every meal to someone who is similarly dependent on alcohol. A building project could do more for cycling than any drive-in movie theatre might have done in the 1960s for driving, and still it would earn no more points towards its green stamp than if it simply provided a wire cage in the basement and a bare concrete room with some showers and lockers.

Perhaps then the answer might be a green trip stamp of approval, which instead of measuring a building's embodied energy and ongoing bills for heating and lighting would focus only on a building's associated transportation? Such a certification programme, called GreenTRIP, has been devised by TransForm, a not-for-profit group in San Francisco that advocates on behalf of developers paying for certification and advice. Unfortunately, because TransForm's focus is purely on emissions (not emissions and health and quick travel and cost-savings and fun – and everything else cycling offers) its accreditation scheme is skewed towards public transport. Despite all the rhetoric and measures on paper that make it look as though Trans-Form is pro-cycling, its accreditation instrument could actually decrease trips by bike. That is because its dominant strategy has been to embed the cost of unlimited access to public transport for residents into the purchase price of apartments in buildings that receive the GreenTRIP certification. Unfortunately, this gives residents an incentive to use public transport: it has already been paid for. We're forced to conclude that TransForm sees bikes as nothing more than devices for cutting walking time to ones nearest hub of motorized public transport where, unfortunately, bikes quickly become nuisance luggage or else nuisance items to store.

If networks of brownfields on flat lands were densely developed and the greenways between them all paved with smooth riding surfaces, and then all the roads were spanned with bicycle flyovers, we would see residents of those parallel bike zones making better time just using their quality bikes than if they used bikes mixed with buses or trains. A moderately fit rider, happy to cruise at between 20 and 30 km/h, would have to live a long way from town, in a very large city, before a train could help shorten his or her daily commute. But environmental groups aren't prepared to entertain such a vision, knowing it would only suit a minority of people, those who don't have an *exertion aversion*.

Environmentalists in government or planning roles will never add real weight to cyclists' concerns, either about infrastructure or, in the case of the present discussion, our preference for buildings that are conducive to coming and going by bike. If a group is more likely to lend us its weight, it would be from the public health sector, and that gives us cause for some optimism. The green agenda may have the hype, but it is for reasons of health and wellbeing that mandatory buildings codes are more often updated.

Flushing toilets, taps and basins, minimum height ceilings, measures to control dampness, access to daylight and air: all these were forced into building codes as part of a long and strong tradition of tightening standards to increase peoples' life expectancy. Somewhere, someday, the case might be made that cycling aids public health as surely as washing ones hands when leaving the toilet. Building codes don't merely provide for the possibility of washing ones hands outside, around a corner, if you really must, because you're a germaphobe. Bathrooms, especially in public buildings, must actively encourage hand washing. Building codes designed to encourage people to cycle and not just make cycling theoretically possible would lessen the burden that sedentary lifestyles place on our hospitals in precisely the same way that building laws on toilets and basins prevent millions of people from being treated each year for diseases spread via faeces. It follows that building codes should not stop at making bicycling possible. They should be geared to making buildings where cycling is as natural as washing your hands.

### To Match or Surpass
### Dutch Standards?

The Dutch make room for bikes on the ground levels of their apartment buildings. Bicycle storerooms come as standard in houses. Their major train stations have vast facilities for safely storing and renting out bikes. Where cyclists in other countries are glad to receive hand-me-down tunnels from industry, Dutch cyclists have tunnels made especially for them. The 1942 Maastunnel, beneath the Maas River in Rotterdam, is a spectacular example, complete with everything from elegant entranceways in the Art Deco style to bicycle escalators. The Dutch build to take cyclists over rivers with just as much flair: the Nescio bicycle bridge in Amsterdam, by Wilkinson Eyre Architects, is as elegant as any bridge Norman Forster or Santiago Calatrava have designed for cars or pedestrians.

Yet despite their conviction to look after bicyclists first, there is something dull and all-too adult about Dutch bicycle structures. To those of us in places that treat bikes as something new and exciting, Dutch buildings for bikes look like Christmas without any tinsel. Their bicycling architecture lacks the exuberance of Washington's Bikestation, for instance, or the conspicuous oomph of BIG's Danish Pavilion at the 2010 Shanghai Expo. Perhaps it is because their bike craze has been going since the late 1800s that the Dutch have not been inclined to build novelty bike bars or cafés like Hopworks Bikebar in Portland. They left it to a British enterprise, Electric

Pedals, to develop the pedal powered cinemas that are now standard items at bicycle festivals. Bikes aren't conspicuously placed in Dutch interior magazines, as they are in counterpart magazines in other countries. It was not a group of Dutch architects, but architects based in Prague, H3T, who developed a bicycle drawn sauna that they promote as yet another contribution to the corpus of green innovations that architects have made since taking on that agenda. In one sense these are the immature gestures of immature bicycling nations that have rediscovered cycling the way educated folk found breast milk again, or cast iron pans that don't have coatings of Teflon. But they also remind people of the magic of pedal power, which is something many Dutch designers have been neglecting to do.

## An Expedient Detour
## in Bicycle Planning

One thing I find magical about cycling is the way circumstance chooses routes for you. You never really plan a route before heading out, or if you do it is unlikely you will adhere to it. It is so easy on a bike to change course that any obstacle or circumstance that could slow you down or make you anxious will inspire some kind of detour. We follow courses of least resistance and routes with less motorized traffic. At most we know where we're heading.

Planning the future of cycling is like planning a ride. We have some vague idea of our destination: cycling Utopia. But we have no idea how we will get there. I suggest we simply get started, the way we get started on bike trips. If we stubbornly adhere to a planned route – copying Dutch history, for instance, or asserting our right to the road – the journey will take us forever and involve unnecessary angst due to conflict with drivers. We will make better time and conserve energy if we take whatever shortcut we happen upon on the way.

Renewed industrial tracts, naturalized urban waterways and former rail routes turned into greenways are providing opportunities to build chains of non-vehicular avenues throughout our cities. I have argued that planning for cycling should focus on these as arterial routes and sites for bicycle oriented development. I am advocating that planners, designers and advocacy groups take the kind of expedient detour we take when we are riding.

When our bike path is blocked by a parked car, we don't get off our bike and try to move it. We just go around. When the street we ideally would use is filled with speeding cars we look for a back street. We don't risk our lives to make a statement. Individually when riding we're used to retreating to space no one else wants and making it into our own cycle space. Committed cyclists go further and let their cycle space determine where they will and won't do their shopping or even work or buy a house. Is it expedient of them to confine their lives to parts of the city that are bike friendly when they could be fighting for cyclists' rights where the fight is most needed? Yes, it is expedient. Let the expediency we apply individually when we are cycling be a cue for the way we tackle some of the impasses facing us as city planners, bicycling advocates and designers. In the end it's our mind-set while cycling that likewise can help us get our cities prepared for the age of the bicycle.

Cycle space in Portland, OR
Photo: Steven Fleming

# Literature

Alta Planning + Design, *The Value of the Bicycle Related Industry in Portland*, September 2008. Available HTTP: www.altaplanning.com (accessed 21 March 2011)

Andersen, Lars Bo, Hans Ole Hein, Peter Schnohr and Marianne Schroll 'All-Cause Mortality Associated With Physical Activity During Leisure Time, Work, Sports, and Cycling to Work', *Archives of Internal Medicine*, vol. 160 (2000)

Antonio Sant'Elia, 'Messaggio', *Niove Tendenze*, 1914

Ballard, J.G., *High-Rise* (London: Jonathan Cape, 1975)

Banham, Reyner, 'A Black Box: The Secret Profession of Architecture', *New Statesman and Society*, 12 October 1990

Banham, Reyner, 'A Grid on Two Farthings', *New Statesman and Society*, 1 November 1963

Banham, Reyner, Los Angeles: *The Architecture of Four Ecologies* (Berkeley: The University of California Press, 2001). Originally published in 1971

Barr, Anne and Peter York, *The Official Sloane Ranger Handbook – The First Guide to What Really Matters in Life*, 10th ed. (London/Sydney: Angus & Robertson, 1982)

Bell, Jonathan, *Carchitecture: When the Car and the City Collide* (Basel: Birkhäuser, 2001)

*Bike Hub*, 'When designing infrastructure for new cyclists, ignore the existing ones, says study', Available HTTP: www.bikehub.co.uk (accessed 11 September 2011)

Brown, Denise Scott and Robert Venturi, 'On Ducks and Decoration', *Architecture Canada* (October 1968)

Buehler, Ralph, John Pucher and Mark Seinen, 'Bicycling Renaissance in North America? An Update and Re-Assessment of Cycling Trends and Policies', *Transportation Research A*, vol. 45 (2011) no. 6

Derrida, Jacques, *Of Grammatology*, translated by Gayatri Chakravorty Spivak (Baltimore: Johns Hopkins University Press, 1976)

Editors of Phaidon Press, *Phaidon Design Classics* (London: Phaidon Press, 2006)

Endo, Shuhei and Hiroyuki Suzuki, *Shuhei Endo: Paramodern Architecture*, edited by Hiroyuki Suzuki, translated by Richard Sadleir (Milan: Electa Architecture, 2003)

Feskanich, Diane, Anne Lusk, Rania Mekary and Walter Willett, 'Bicycle Riding, Walking, and Weight Gain in Premenopausal Women', *Archives of Internal Medicine*, vol. 170 (2010) no. 12

Freud, Sigmund, 'Metapsychological Supplement to the Theory of Dreams' (1916), in: *General Psychological Theory* (New York: Macmillan, 1963)

Geller, Roger, free to download lecture, Available harangue.lecture.unimelb.edu.au (accessed 25 October 2010)

Giedion, Sigfried, Space, *Time and Architecture: The Growth of a New Tradition* (Cambridge, MA: Harvard University Press, 1967)

La, Grace and Winy Maas (eds.), *Skycar City: A Pre-emptive History* (Barcelona: Actar, 2007)

Le Corbusier, *Towards a New Architecture* (London: Architectural Press Limited, 1927)

Loos, Adolf, 'Ornament and Crime', in: Ludwig Munx and Gustav Kunstler (eds.), *Adolf Loos: Pioneer of Modern Architecture* (London: Thames and Hudson, 1966). First published 1908

Marinetti, Filippo Tommaso, 'Futurist Manifestor', in: R.W. Flint (ed.), *Marinetti: Selected Writings* (New York: Farrar, Straus and Giroux, 1972). First published in Le Figaro, 20 February 1909

Noland, Robert B., 'Perceived Risk and Modal Choice: Risk Compensation in Transportation Systems', *Accident Analysis and Prevention*, vol. 27 (1995) no. 4

Peltzman, S., 'The Effects of Automobile Safety Regulation', *Journal of Political Economy*, vol. 83 (1975) no. 4

Pevsner, Nikolaus, *An Outline of European Architecture*, 6th ed. (Harmondsworth, UK: Penguin Books, 1960)

Pooley, Colin G. (corresponding author), 'Understanding Walking and Cycling, Summary of Key Findings and Recommendations' (2011), 11. Available HTTP: www.apho.org.uk (accessed 16 February 2012)

Roberts, Steven K., *Computing Across America: The Bicycle Odyssey of a High-Tech Nomad* (Medford, NJ: Information Today, 1988)

Rossi, Aldo, *The Architecture of the City*, translated by Diane Ghirardo and Joan Ockman (Cambridge, MA: MIT Press, 1984). First published in 1966 as *L'architettura della città*

Ruskin, John, Lecture IV, 'The Influence of Imagination in Architecture', in: *The Two Paths: Being Lectures on Art and Its Application to Decoration and Manufacture*, delivered in 1858-1859 (London: G. Allen, 1906)

Singapore's Land and Transport Authority's website, www.onemotoring.com.sg (accessed 16 March 2012)

Stevens, Gary, *The Favoured Circle*, (Cambridge, MA: MIT Press, 2002)

The City of Minneapolis Community Planning and Economic Development Department, 'Midtown Greenway Land Use Development Plan', 23 February 2007. Available HTTP: www.minneapolismn.gov (accessed 16 February 2012)

Vidler, Anthony, 'The Third Typology', in: Kate Nesbitt (ed.), *Theorizing a New Agenda for Architecture: An Anthology of Architectural Theory 1965-1995* (New York: Princeton Architectural Press, 1996)

Wigley, Mark, 'Prosthetic Theory: The Disciplining of Architecture', Assemblage (1991) no. 15

Wittkower, Rudloph, *Architectural Principles in the Age of Humanism* (New York: W.W. Norton, 1971)

Wolfe, Tom, *From Bauhaus to Our House* (New York: Farrar, Straus & Giroux, 1981)

# Credits

Much of this book was researched during a travelling sabbatical from the University of Newcastle, when fellow believers in cycling all over the world shared their time freely with me. In Singapore, that was Jacinta Sonja and (via email) Tom Keeble. In Rotterdam architects at West-8 and MVRDV generously explained their firms' approaches. Tours were arranged for me in Portland by Kirsten Kaufman, Jennifer Marsicek, Emiliano Jordan and Kenneth Wheeler. Brent Norsman oriented me to the cycling and architectural scene in Chicago, and has kindly provided photographs for that city portrait. I spent the greatest two weeks in New York with architect, blogger and cyclist David Holowka who introduced me as well to the amazing Charles Komanoff. I spent a great morning at BIG's NYC office too, getting an inside scoop on the workings of this most inspirational practice. Dr Anne Lusk provided me with a brief, but incredibly rewarding visiting position at the Harvard School of Public Health. The most rollicking, yet illuminating time was spent in Copenhagen with Mikael Colville-Andersen, whose photos may have helped you decide to purchase this book. Thanks in Copenhagen as well to Lars Gemzøe.

Companions in this enterprise range from old friends to generous followers of my blog: Gus Potts, Robert Milan, Robert Cooper, Brendon Lowndes, Angelina Russo, Paul Squire, Bernard Hockings, Brian Jones, Thomas Hatton, Jasmine Richardson and Ben Ewald. The greatest thanks of course go to Kerry, my wife, and my sons Aquinas and Atlas, all of whom tolerate my obsession with cycling and all the time I spend away overseas, or just away in my mind.

More than 80 organisations and individuals contributed toward the production costs of this book through a crowd funding website. My special thanks go to Paul van Bellen of Gazelle Bicycles Australia for his company's substantial donation. I am also grateful for the encouragement shown to me by the staff of the School of Architecture and Design at the University of Tasmania, who have partnered with us on this project and have proved as mad about cycling as I am.

I would lastly like to thank nai010 publishers and my editor Mehgan Bakhuizen who saw the thread of sense amidst the wild speculation to help produce a book even I am now able to follow. Thank you Mehgan for giving this project all your talent and such close attention. Previously her colleagues Marcel Witvoet and Eelco van Welie recognised the potential in my first drafts and steered me on a path to a book I can take far greater pride in thanks to their wisdom.

Steven Fleming

The book Cycle Space is in association with the University of Tasmania, Australia, and made possible through generous support from the Netherlands Architecture Fund and Gazelle Bicycles Australia

With thanks to:
BikeWise Australia
Cycling Promotion Fund
Christopher Jones, Bicycles Network Australia
Donovan McMurray
Robert Milan
Morgans Bicycles
ORTRE Limited
Warren Salomon, Sustainable Transport Consultants Pty Ltd
Carrie Sze, whydyouride.info
Cara Wiseman

Illustration credits
Kaspar Astrup Schröder 126
Iwan Baan 73
Reyner Banham, *Design by Choice* (New York: Rizzoli, 1981) 108
Calfee Design 73
Mikael Colville-Andersen cover, 12-13, 15-17, 29, 36-40, 46, 58-63, 66, 118, 120-123
Peter Cossey, Shweeb 22
Steven Fleming 4, 6, 6, 14-15, 22, 29, 39, 46, 66, 73, 88, 98-103, 119, 120, 142-143, 158-163, 166, 174
Chris Hardwicke 131
Tom Hatton 148
Alex Ivanov 73
Michael Ubbesen Jakobsen 66
JDS Architects 73
Kronan Bikes 126
Patrick Lichfield / Foster + Partners 108
Robert Milan 148
National Archives of the Netherlands / Spaarnestad Photo 78-83
Nomadic Research Labs photo archives 108
Brent Norseman 138-141
Gus Potts 78-83
Gabriella Sanderson 22
State Library of New South Wales 78
Sunrider 92
Ken Wheeler, Renovo Bikes 66

Texts
Steven Fleming
Copy editing
D'Laine Camp
Design
75B
Lithography and printing
NPN Drukkers, Breda
Production
Mehgan Bakhuizen, nai010 publishers, Rotterdam
Publisher
nai010 publishers, Rotterdam
Cover photo
Mikael Colville-Andersen

nai010 publishers is an internationally orientated publisher specialized in developing, producing and distributing books in the fields of architecture, urbanism, art and design.
www.nai010.com

Available in North, South and Central America through Artbook | D.A.P.,
155 Sixth Avenue 2nd Floor
New York, NY 10013-1507
tel +1 212 627 1999
fax +1 212 627 9484
dap@dapinc.com

Available in the United Kingdom and Ireland through Art Data
12 Bell Industrial Estate
50 Cunnington Street
London W4 5HB
tel +44 208 747 1061
fax +44 208 742 2319
orders@artdata.co.uk

Printed and bound in the Netherlands

ISBN 978-94-6208-004-1